WITHDRAWN

WITHDRAWN

CHINA'S WARTIME POLITICS
1937-1944

Issued under the auspices of
International Secretariat
Institute of Pacific Relations

CHINA'S
WARTIME POLITICS
1937-1944

BY

LAWRENCE K. ROSINGER

PRINCETON
PRINCETON UNIVERSITY PRESS
1 9 4 5

This book is complete and unabridged in contents, and is manufactured in strict conformity with Government regulations for saving paper.

SECOND EDITION, JANUARY 1945

TO MY PARENTS

PREFACE

The increasing public interest (sometimes anxious interest) on the part of the people in many parts of the Western world in the political and military developments in Free China is important for several reasons. On the one hand it shows a growing awareness of the vital role which the Chinese armies and Allied forces operating in China may play in the final defeat of Japan. On the other hand it evidences a belated and sometimes unbalanced knowledge of the fearful real burden which seven years of war, blockade and inflation have laid on the Chinese people and government. With that knowledge there is also some realization of the immense tasks which lie ahead if China is to be not only rehabilitated to her political and economic position of 1937 but also set upon the road to far-reaching economic reconstruction and political reform and thus enabled to fulfil the international responsibilities of a major power in the postwar world. Few people will dispute the urgent need of having China as a great Asiatic nation included as an effective, and not merely a nominal, member of the Big Four or Big Five powers. For that reason there cannot be too much study on the part of Westerners of how best China, so sorely handicapped these past seven years, can be aided to develop the material resources and the political and social mechanisms which will permit her to pull her full weight with the other great nations.

In that process of study it will be found essential to examine the political development of Free China during the war years. For despite the conservatism of Chinese life and the persistence of age-old social patterns and habits, the violent upheavals of the war with its vast displacement of population and economic life have forced political changes which are bound to influence the whole plan of Chinese post-war government and economic development. The full impact of these political changes can only be dimly glimpsed as yet. Their real effect may only become clear when the constant pressure of Japanese armies has ceased and when the Chinese government begins to re-establish its authority in eastern and northern China and in such restored territories as Manchuria and Formosa. Undoubt-

edly the difficulties and new responsibilities which these tasks
will present will necessitate rapid political changes to meet
varying circumstances and one cannot assume that the present
political practices of Free China today will all be continued.
Nevertheless the influences of the political groupings, the habits
of administration, the ideologies which have grown up in the
war years will not suddenly disappear but will make themselves
felt in many ways and for many years.

The present book attempts to sketch, only in brief outline,
some of these major wartime political developments in Free
China and to show their connection with the course of the war
itself and with the accompanying economic disorganization
which it has brought. It does not pretend to be a treatise on
Chinese government and politics or an analysis of the course of
the war in China. It does not attempt to discuss the intricacies
of Chinese provincial and local politics and the personalities
involved in them. Finally it omits any detailed account of
China's relations during the war period with her neighboring
and Allied nations, though it is fully realized that this question
(particularly that aspect of it affecting military and economic
aid to China) has many important bearings on political developments inside Free China. The book has been purposely limited
to a narrative of the major events in national political and war-
time administration, in the belief that such an account, supported by pertinent documents, may be of value to Western
friends of China in studying some of the vexing problems of
peace in the Far East. At a later date the I.P.R. Secretariat expects to issue another volume, by a well-qualified Chinese
writer, on some of the more detailed problems of internal administration and reconstruction in the new China.

In sponsoring the present book the I.P.R. Secretariat does not
assume responsibility for statements of fact or opinion expressed
therein. For all such statements the author alone is responsible.

W. L. HOLLAND

New York   Research Secretary
July 1944   Institute of Pacific Relations

NOTE: The second edition is identical with the first in pagination. A post-
script has been added on p. 61, a few corrections have been made in the text
and index, and slight verbal changes on pp. 36, 47, and 53 to allow for new
footnotes. There have been no alterations in the documentary section.

CONTENTS

DOCUMENTS

CHINA'S WARTIME POLITICS
1937-1944

CHAPTER I

THE POLITICAL BACKGROUND

The Roots of Nationalism

When China's national resistance began in 1937 almost a century had passed since Western armed power first breached the walls of the Manchu Empire. Many far-reaching, progressive changes had taken place in that time, but modern China had still not achieved genuine independence. It was clearly not a colony or protectorate of any foreign nation. Nor was its policy dictated by the united pressure of a combination of powers. Yet, parts of China—such as Formosa and Hongkong—had long been foreign possessions, and the vast region of Manchuria had fallen to Japan only a few years before. Moreover, there were various long-term leases of Chinese territory as well as so-called concessions—areas of foreign residence and influence in some of the leading cities. In Shanghai, for example, a predominantly foreign Municipal Council governed the International Settlement, the country's most important financial, industrial and commercial center.

Foreign power was more than a matter of territory. It affected the functions of government as well as the scope and nature of Chinese development. Foreign troops were on Chinese soil, and foreign shipping dominated China's waters. The system of extraterritoriality, which removed leading groups of foreigners from the jurisdiction of Chinese courts, gave many alien businessmen an advantage over their Chinese competitors. Even more important in hampering the growth of industry was China's lack of power to fix its own tariff. Customs autonomy, it is true, had been granted by the powers, but Japanese pressure after the invasion of Manchuria in 1931 prevented the adoption of a fully independent tariff policy. In fact, many of the gains made by the Chinese nationalist movement in the 1920's were more than cancelled out in the following decade by loss of sovereignty to Japan. An important shift in the character of China's foreign relations was therefore taking place: although special western privileges continued to be regarded as a burden, they were overshadowed increasingly by Japan's active policy of expansion, which threatened the existence of almost every section of the Chinese nation. This is easily seen from a brief examination of the facts.

In 1937 the Chinese middle class was still very weak politically, for modern industry and banking were confined to small areas and were not primarily under Chinese control. Textiles and other articles of light industry constituted the bulk of factory production. Partly because of foreign influence, Chinese banks invested little of their capital in the field of industrial development. Instead of concerning themselves largely with production as such, they used their funds to purchase government bonds, urban real estate and agricultural produce, and to promote communication facilities. An important part of the middle class participated in a more or less subordinate capacity in foreign-directed enterprises. With so large a personal interest in China's existing status, this group sometimes wavered in its spirit of nationalism. Yet, China's merchants, bankers and industrialists as a whole came to realize that Japanese aggression was incompatible with their survival even in their existing inferior position.

A relatively small working class—principally factory workers, craftsmen, coolies and maritime laborers—lived in the great cities of the coast and Yangtze Valley area, while a larger body of rural handicraft and farm workers carried on an almost separate existence in the interior. The conditions in factories and workshops were reminiscent of the early days of the Industrial Revolution in the West. Child labor was common, the working day long and wages low. Large numbers of women were employed, and sanitary and safety measures were in a most rudimentary stage. The organized trade-union movement—a powerful factor in the nationalism of the mid-twenties—had been in large part broken or driven underground by the Central government after 1927. But the spirit of nationalism survived among the more advanced industrial workers and expressed itself in rising anti-Japanese sentiment in the 1930's, for they increasingly felt that the improvement of their own position was linked with the creation of an independent China.

Lower middle class groups in the cities, including shopkeepers and students, were also thwarted by China's inability to develop freely. The evasion of the Chinese tariff by Japanese smugglers ruined many small Chinese merchants, mainly in North China, while the political power that accompanied the smuggling threatened the centers of education. The students, who were acutely aware of the contrast between China's status and that of the powers, were also in an excellent position to furnish nationalist leadership. Better prepared than the average peasant or worker to think about the country's problems, they were far more willing than the average businessman to assume the risks involved in patriotic action. Large numbers of the students saw clearly that China's future depended first of all on the creation of a sovereign nation, following progressive paths at home and abroad.

City groups, however, were only a small part of the population, for eight out of ten Chinese still depended on the soil for a living. On millions of tiny farms, debt-ridden peasant owners and tenants, together with those who rented land to supplement their own little holdings struggled to earn a living. Absentee landlordism and tenancy often went hand in hand, especially near the great cities, where many landlords lived on receipts from the countryside. Capitalism in agriculture hardly existed in view of the intensive use of human labor on extremely small holdings.

These social conditions were part of an outmoded land system under which the peasantry was caught in a web of rent, usury and taxes, with the landlords often acting simultaneously as rent-collectors, merchants, money-lenders and officials. Local rule was almost completely under the control of important landowners who established a most careful watch over the activities of the peasants. As a result of this situation, the latter, at least in the territory of the Central government, had little to say in popular discussion about the menace of Japanese aggression. But since the beginning of resistance they have often shown in unmistakable fashion that they identify their own future with defeat of the enemy.

Of all groups in China, the rural landlords, gentry and officials had the greatest stake in the existing order. Even to the most forward-looking among them the problems presented by the country's backwardness were likely to appear theoretical as long as rents, taxes and interest could be collected. Not only would genuine modernization have involved far-reaching adjustments on their part; but, specifically, a war of resistance against

Japan threatened to bring fighting into the fields, upset the customary relationships of the countryside, and perhaps increase the power of the peasantry. Provincially-minded individuals among the gentry were not likely to take alarm as long as Japanese aggression appeared to be directed against the national power or some region of the country other than their own. Yet, it was becoming clear by 1937 that all hopes for local safety from the invader were an illusion. Moreover, even for the rural leaders, many of whose children took part in student movements, there existed motives of a nationalist character—sentiments which were influenced by the more determined, patriotic reaction of other groups in the cities of China.

It is clear that in 1937 the great majority of the Chinese people had one common need: independence from Japanese control which, in aggressiveness and immediacy, far outweighed any other outside influence. It would be false to suggest that this situation was grasped logically and in its many aspects by large masses of the population, or even by most of China's leaders, but it was appreciated sufficiently to make resistance possible. Once the die was cast, war itself became the supreme teacher: despite the wavering of some groups and individuals the country realized more and more that its existence was at stake.

The Growth of Modern Government.

Chinese nationalism achieved its first success with the overthrow of the Manchu Empire in 1911, but even the wisest of the revolutionaries did not realize that the mere assembling of a Parliament could not make of China a modern nation. The political upheaval, so pregnant with consequences for the future, had the immediate effect of substituting for the Manchu government a Chinese regime that soon proved to be unequal to its tasks. Sun Yat-sen, the great nationalist leader, and his political party, the Kuomintang, were quickly driven from power. The dissolution of the weak Manchu controls over a vast decentralized country allowed the forces of provincialism to emerge in full strength. Local and regional deputies of the former regime paid lip-service to the Republic, but became, in fact, warlords and leaders of corruption. China entered a period of unprincipled civil war.

Yet, counter-forces were appearing. World War I encouraged the rise of modern industry and of Chinese industrialists and financiers, thus strengthening the middle class basis for a nationalist movement. At the same time a modern working class began to develop in some numbers, labor unions were formed, and the patriotic student movement rose to new heights. The October Revolution in Russia also had considerable influence on Chinese nationalist circles, which were gratified by the Soviet renunciation of various Tsarist privileges in China and attracted by Soviet declarations against the colonial system. In the spring of 1921 a Chinese Communist Party was formed. Within little more than two years Sun Yat-sen, then the leader of a Kuomintang government centered at Canton, had decided on cooperation with the Chinese Communists and an alliance with the U.S.S.R.

The First National Congress of the Kuomintang, held at the beginning of 1924, gave its approval to this move. The party was reorganized, and its platform was broadened to include a greater appeal to the peasant and labor movements. At the same time, although the Communists retained their own party organization, they were admitted to membership in the Kuomintang, and three Communists were appointed to its Central Executive Committee. The Kuomintang now became, in effect, a nationalist alliance. This was in keeping with Sun Yat-sen's deep conviction that all groups in China were suffering from some type of oppression and that all should therefore cooperate.

Sun's death in March 1925 was a most serious loss, but the nationalist movement stemmed from forces greater than any one man. Millions of ordinary Chinese were beginning to participate in the struggle for the goals he had proposed: national independence, political democracy and economic security (known as San Min Chu I, or Three Principles of the People). The period, 1925-27, was one of upheaval, marked by widespread strikes, great stirrings of the peasantry and a powerful mass movement against foreign control, all of which were aided by the Kuomintang and its government at Canton. Now a new figure came to the fore: General Chiang Kai-shek, who had worked with Sun Yat-sen and had become Canton's outstanding military leader. In March 1926, while still at Canton, Chiang removed Wang Ching-wei and other left-wing members of the Kuomintang from party leadership and also curbed sharply the governmental influence of the Communists. This was the first sign of a break in the united front, but the situation did not deteriorate further at the time.

In July 1926, with Chiang as Commander-in-chief, there began the famous Northern Expedition, an attempt of the nationalist nucleus in the south to unify the country by destroying the power of the warlords in other areas and ending foreign control. Welcomed everywhere by the people, the armies from Canton soon took over large sections of south and central China. Toward the end of the year the capital was transferred to the important industrial center of Wuhan (comprising Hankow, Hanyang and Wuchang) on the Yangtze. These developments were greatly facilitated by strikes and peasant uprisings in the rear of the warlord forces. Many strikes occurred also in Kuomintang China, as well as a significant expansion of peasant and labor unions. At first the peasants secured reductions in rents and taxes; later there was much seizure and redivision of land. The Communists, active in these movements, increased their strength, although remaining far weaker than the non-Communist majority of the Kuomintang.

With the nationalist seizure of Shanghai late in March 1927 the united front split wide open, as a powerful coalition consisting of the right wing of the Kuomintang in combination with outstanding industrial and financial interests in the lower Yangtze valley moved to suppress the mass movement. The concomitant growth of nationalist control and the popular desire for reform had brought to the surface a fundamental problem: under what type of government was a unified China to be organized? The conservatives, led by Chiang Kai-shek, seem to have concluded that they had attained as much of their objectives as they could at the moment without risking loss of their leadership to the liberals and left-wing groups. But an important additional factor in influencing their attitude and making possible their success was the position taken by the foreign powers who were alarmed at many aspects of the popular movement and desired a change in nationalist policy. This made it very difficult to go forward with the unification of China unless the popular movement was further strengthened.

The new regime at Nanking controlled the most important section of China and ultimately was recognized by the powers. It was supported by the Shanghai bankers, as well as land owners and businessmen in many areas, and various local and provincial warlords. It had behind it not only the Kuomintang organization and the prestige of Sun Yat-sen's name, but also the allegiance of military and political circles that found it expedient to jump on the bandwagon. On the other hand, the weakness of Nanking and Chiang-Kai-shek at the time should not be underestimated. The lower Yangtze valley, although important, was not all of China, and recognition by the powers was a thin reed to lean on and no guarantee against future aggression. The support of wealthy Chinese was important, but there was also the problem of dealing with the mass movement of peasants and workers. As for the alliances with the various warlords, these were purely marriages of convenience.

With the occupation of Peking—soon renamed Peiping—in June 1928 and the pledging of allegiance by the Manchurian warlord, Chang Hsueh-liang, in the same year, all China was nominally under Nanking's control. In October 1928 the Organic Law of the National Government of the Republic of China was proclaimed. It established a one-party administration of the Kuomintang, a type of rule not new in China, but markedly different from the democratic practice and theory of the party during the years in which it had embraced all sections of the nationalist movement. Nanking explained the existing system of government by citing the view of Sun Yat-sen that after military unification China would have to pass through a period of "political tutelage" in which the people would be prepared for self-government. Yet it was clear that policy was being determined by more pressing considerations than the words of a dead leader. This was indicated by Nanking's determined effort to consolidate its position through suppression not simply of the Communists, but also of the popular democratic movement and, in the last analysis, all critical groups. Under the new conditions of civil war the Kuomintang was transformed into a party consisting chiefly of officials, persons wishing to enter the government service, and representatives of the dominant economic groups.

The new regime functioned through many governmental and extra-governmental bodies, not coordinated in a logical system. There was, first of all, the formal administrative set-up which, following the theories of Sun Yat-sen, contained five main departments (known in Chinese as Yuan). These were the Executive, Legislative and Judicial Yuan—copied in name from the three branches of the United States government—and the Control and Examination Yuan, created to supervise the conduct of officials and take charge of civil service examinations, respectively. The Executive Yuan, which included various bureaus called Ministries, was sometimes spoken of as the Cabinet and its President as the Premier, although these were not official designations.

Secondly, there was the Nationalist Party—the Kuomintang—a hierarchy of organs, leading up to the Central Supervisory Committee (also known as the Central Control Committee) and the Central Executive Committee. Although this system had been modelled upon that of the Communist Party in the Soviet Union—at the time of the Kuomintang's reorganization in 1924—it was maintained even after the split with the Left. In terms of practical politics it would be fruitless to make distinctions between the powers of the official political party and the official administrative organization. The Kuomintang interpenetrated the regime at innumerable points, since many of the principal officials were leaders of the party. Moreover, it was at sessions of the Central Executive Committee (or its smaller Standing Committee) that some of the fundamental policies of the government were shaped. On the other hand, persons who were not Kuomintang members, but were nevertheless influential, were often appointed to highly important posts. The regime was guided by many forces of which the Kuomintang and the government organs were only two, furnishing the framework, but only part of the substance of official action.

Behind and above both the party and administration was the army—or, more exactly, the armies. China then, as before, was being ruled by military men who, with the support of landed and urban interests, formed a series of shifting coalitions. Sometimes they engaged in war (the Central government's war with Feng Yu-hsiang and Yen Hsi-shan in 1930 was a sanguinary affair). At other times they found the mere exhibition of potential force enough to bring about political change. There was, however, at least one important difference between the situation in 1928 and in the previous years of warlordism: Chiang Kai-shek had more concentrated armed power at his command than any general since the Manchus, and his regime was an outgrowth of the nationalist movement.

Meanwhile Nanking had entered a period of civil war with

the Communists. In August 1927 several Kuomintang officers of Communist views led a successful revolt of Nationalist troops at Nanchang, and a Hunan peasant uprising during the following month produced the first units of what later became the Chinese Red Army. In November 1927 the first Soviet in China was set up on the Hunan-Kiangsi border, and in November 1931 a Central Soviet Government was established in Kiangsi province, with Mao Tse-tung as Chairman, while Chu Teh held the post of Commander-in-Chief of the Chinese Red Army. The Soviets followed a far-reaching policy of land distribution under which the holdings of the rich were divided among the poorer peasants. With other factors, such as mass education, political instruction, and elective councils, this served as the basis for a military strategy of guerrilla warfare in fighting the Central forces.

One problem faced by Nanking was whether a government that was not yet fully independent could successfully wage civil war against strong internal opponents. The question appeared theoretical for several years, but the Japanese invasion of Manchuria in September 1931 indicated that a choice might ultimately have to be made between national resistance and civil strife. For the moment the decision was in favor of non-resistance to Japan, with the National Government limiting itself to appeals to the League of Nations for aid. Under Central Government orders, the Manchurian armies of Chang Hsueh-liang soon retired south of the Great Wall. Whatever Chinese resistance took place was largely local and spontaneous. During these early post-1931 years, two short-lived revolts involving among others some of the more liberal elements within the Kuomintang gave expression to Chinese sentiment against the appeasement of Japan. The first, in the north, was headed in the beginning by General Feng Yu-hsiang and then briefly continued by General Fang Chen-wu. More significant was the revolt of the Nineteenth Route Army, of Shanghai fame, which broke out in Fukien late in 1933. Headed by General Tsai Ting-kai and a strong group of liberal Kuomintang leaders, this movement, though speedily crushed, was prophetic of future events in the negotiations which it initiated with the Communists for a united front under the principle of resistance to Japan.

For a period the military pressure on the Chinese Soviets was reduced and they were able to expand their territories, but in October 1933 Nanking launched its fifth anti-Communist campaign, in the course of which, aided by the advice of a German military mission, it mobilized nearly one million men and employed a modern air force. Early in 1934 the Kiangsi Communists decided to leave the province and move to a new base in the northwest. Their departure began in October. By July 1935 they had effected a juncture in Szechwan with Communist units previously established in the southern districts of that province. A few months later Red Army vanguards reached Shensi province in the northwest, although the bulk of the troops did not reach this area until 1936. While Nanking had forced the Communists to leave their base in Central China, the main objective of wiping them out had not been achieved.

In the course of this drive, however, Nanking won new power in a number of provinces, especially Hunan, Kweichow, Yunnan and Szechwan. In all of them Central authority had been nominally supreme and actually weak. But the poor performance—and even complete lack of resistance—of the local forces whose areas the Communists entered enabled Nanking to send in its own troops. Though intended in part for use against the Communists, the Central armies were sometimes employed to a greater extent against the provincial authorities. The situation was one in which both national and local leaders were jockeying for political position on the basis of the anti-Communist campaign.

The pattern of Nanking's subordination of the provinces was similar in the various areas. First the Communists approached or entered a province, threatening the existing local and national authority. Central troops were then dispatched in reply. After a period of preparation by Nanking representatives, Chiang Kai-shek would go to the provincial capital by plane and announce his intention to improve local conditions. The work of provincial reorganization would now begin in earnest, the degree of change depending upon whether the local authorities were strong or weak. The Central objectives were: control of the provincial armed forces, reorganization of the military and civilian personnel of the provincial government, and the extension of Central economic influence (through the establishment of branches of the Central Bank of China, the substitution of national for local currency and national participation in taxes and railway revenues). While this process was going on, the Communists would probably have left the province, but the Central troops remained.

These developments were superficially favorable to the conception of a strong National government. And they were accompanied, especially during the period from the end of 1935 until the outbreak of war in 1937, by the building of new roads and railways, important currency and tax reforms, and other forward-looking economic measures that strengthened the Central power. They occurred, however, at a time of increasing Japanese aggression and, in effect, were outweighed by the activities of the invaders. This was all the more true since the diversion of China's energies in continued civil war was incompatible with national resistence to aggression. As long as Chinese fought among themselves their country was certain to be the prey of Japan.

National Resistance to Aggression

In the fall of 1935 China began to emerge from its seeming passivity and popular demand became more insistent that the government abandon civil war and appeasement for a policy of unity and resistance. That a turning point was approaching was not immediately apparent, since Japan seemed on the verge of seizing China's five northern provinces, containing approximately one-sixth of the country's population. Moreover, the regime continued to follow a weak diplomatic policy, while certain Chinese groups sought to reach an agreement with the aggressor. In October 1935, for example, a mission of Chinese financiers, merchants and industrialists, some of whom were closely linked with the government banking system, visited Japan for this purpose.

Then, on November 1, 1935, at a meeting of the Kuomintang Central Executive Committee, an attempt was made to assassinate Wang Ching-wei, who was Foreign Minister and President of the Executive Yuan. This attack on the man most closely associated in the public mind with the policy of yielding to Japan was a significant development. At the Congress that followed Chiang Kai-shek enunciated the official foreign policy in these words: "We shall not forsake peace until there is no hope for peace. We shall not talk lightly of sacrifice until we are driven to the last extremity which makes sacrifice inevitable."

China, he said, should "practice forbearance in facing issues not of a fundamental nature" and "seek harmonious international relations provided there is no violation of our sovereignty."[1]

On November 1 the Students' Self-Government Association of eleven colleges, universities and middle schools in Peiping and Tientsin had petitioned the Kuomintang session for freedom of speech, assembly and association and the prohibition of illegal arrests of students. A powerful popular movement soon developed against Japanese plans to create an "autonomous" north China. On December 9, 1935 the storm broke. In an essentially spontaneous demonstration, whose only leadership came from the newly formed Peiping Students' Union, thousands of students marched in the streets of that city displaying patriotic banners and shouting slogans. They demanded that the government announce its foreign policy, make public all previous negotiations, grant civil liberties and cease civil war in order to fight the common enemy, Japan. Within two weeks not a university town in China was untouched by student activity in support of national unity and resistance. At the same time a national patriotic movement was developing that included persons of all classes, occupations, political sympathies and regions.

Unions of lawyers were formed. Journalists organized and petitioned the government for freedom of speech and press. Patriotic action was stirred up among the city laborers. In Shanghai a Workers' Anti-Japanese National Salvation Association was formed, but was declared illegal. On May 29-30, 1936, student delegates inaugurated the Students' National Salvation Union; and on May 31 almost half a year of activity reached a climax when sixty delegates, representing more than fifty national salvation groups and twenty other bodies, inaugurated the All-China Federation of National Salvation Unions. The decision was reached that the Federation should remain apart from all political parties and serve as the organization of the Chinese patriotic front. The conference manifesto concluded with this program:

"1. That all parties and groups immediately put an end to civil war;

"2. That all parties and groups immediately free the political prisoners in their custody;

[1] *The China Year Book, 1936* (Shanghai) pp. 169-170.

"3. That all parties and groups immediately send formal delegates, through the National Salvation Front of the People, to begin joint negotiations, so as to formulate the joint anti-enemy program and to build a united anti-enemy political power;

"4. That the National Salvation Front of the People will guarantee with all the force at its disposal the faithful fulfillment of the anti-enemy program by any and all parties and groups;

"5. That the National Salvation Front of the People will with all the forces at its disposal, use sanctions against any party and group that violates the joint anti-enemy program, and acts to weaken the united strength against the enemy."[2]

The rise of the patriotic movement pointed toward a restoration of the national unity that had been broken in 1927. The chief problem was to bring the civil war between the Kuomintang and the Communists to a halt. The first step on the Communist side had been taken on August 1, 1935 with the publication of an appeal to the nation to resist Japan and save the country. At the end of the month another Communist statement had been issued. Addressed to "men and women in all walks of life—labor, industry, agriculture, military affairs, politics, commerce and education," the manifesto was phrased in the language of nationalism, not of class warfare. It urged the "formation of a united national defense government," a provisional organ which would call together the representatives of all China to discuss the problems of resistance in concrete fashion.[3] Yet, both August declarations had been directed not toward the Nanking government, but against it and the Japanese. The Kuomintang reaction was to consider this modification of Communist policy a maneuver designed to secure popular support. The civil war went on, and in October 1935 Chiang Kai-shek's headquarters at Sian offered high rewards for the capture of important Communist leaders—for example, 100,000 Chinese dollars for Mao Tse-tung alive, 80,000 if dead.

Despite its rapid development in the early part of 1936, the popular movement toward a national united front had important weaknesses. First of all, it lacked close-knit organization and a single leadership. Secondly, in the absence of a strong liberal wing in the Kuomintang, it was difficult for the salvation movement to reach the members or armed forces of that party except through the recognized leaders—the very men who were

[2] For full text of the manifesto, see Appendix, pp. 86-93.
[3] For full text, see Appendix, pp. 63-69.

pursuing the foreign and domestic policies that were under attack. Moreover, the Communists found that, despite their new proposals, the retention for the most part of the old agrarian and political methods of the Chinese Soviets greatly hampered them in establishing cooperation with other anti-Japanese groups.

In 1935-36 the Soviet region comprised a number of counties in the Shensi-Kansu-Ninghsia border region of the Northwest. It was here, first at Paoan and later at Yenan, both in Shensi province, that the Chinese Soviet Republic had established its new capital. The economic and political changes that had then been initiated included: redistribution of land and livestock belonging to landlords; revision and reduction of taxes; abolition of usury and limitation of interest rates; and official extension of credits and other aid to the peasants. The smallest political unit was the village Soviet, above which there stood in ascending order the district, county, provincial and central Soviets. Universal suffrage existed for those over sixteen, but tenant farmers, handicraft workers and rural workers received greater representation than other groups in elections to the Soviets. According to Edgar Snow, the peasants in the Soviet area showed great enthusiasm: "I noticed also that most of them talked about the Soviets as *womenti chengfu*—'our government'—and this struck me as something new in rural China."[4]

Partly in response to outside demands for change, the Communists announced in March 1936 that the Soviet Workers' and Peasants' Republic had been renamed the Soviet People's Republic—a title less disturbing to many persons. Willingness was expressed to abolish all taxes on lower middle class persons, to help them in their businesses and to give them greater political privileges. Taxation on merchants and industrialists, it was declared, had been reduced, and their property was no longer to be confiscated. Moreover, changes in land policy were promised.

Equally important were statements made by Mao Tse-tung in an interview at this time. While sharply attacking Nanking's policy toward Japan and declaring that the Communists would not permit any action against the Chinese Red Army, he stated that the struggle with Chiang Kai-shek had not been waged against him as an individual. He pledged that if Chiang's army

---

[4] Edgar Snow, *Red Star Over China* (New York, Garden City Publishing Co., 1939), p. 215.

or any other army ceased fighting the Red forces, the latter would at once halt military operations and cooperate with their former enemy in an anti-Japanese war. Regardless of party differences and previous attitudes, he said, the Soviets set no condition for unity other than joint struggle against Japan. These declarations indicated the gradual realization by the Communists that, without the inclusion of the Nanking government and China's most important leader, Chiang Kai-shek, there could be no effective unity against Japan.

Although Kuomintang-Communist unity was not established at this time, greater harmony was soon achieved on another front. After 1927 there had been a split between Nanking and the southern provinces whose political and economic center lay at Canton in Kwangtung province. Though sometimes a conflict over principle, differences related chiefly to questions of power. Following the Japanese invasion of Manchuria a reconciliation between Nanking and some of the southern leaders had occurred. But there continued to exist at Canton the Southwestern Political Council, an autonomous organization which was neither so strong that it could break away from Nanking completely nor so weak that it could not maintain itself. Yet, for all its intransigence, the Southwest gradually was hemmed in through the neutralization of Yunnan and the extension of Central influence over Kweichow and Szechwan. The Southwest was coming more and more to consist of only two provinces—Kwangsi and Kwangtung.

Verbally the Southwest adopted an anti-Japanese policy. On the part of Chen Chi-tang, chief warlord of Kwangtung, this was merely a propaganda device to use against Nanking. But in Kwangsi his allies, Generals Li Tsung-jen and Pai Tsung-hsi, permitted the student and National Salvation movements to develop freely. Late in May 1936 relations with Nanking reached a crisis when the Southwestern leaders issued a manifesto to the nation, urging, in effect, war on Japan, in order to prevent the increase of Japanese troops in North China. They also declared that they wished to send their own forces northward against the invaders.

But before the Kwangtung-Kwangsi movement was two weeks old it began to break up. Southwestern delegates participated in a specially convened meeting of the Kuomintang Central Executive Committee at which Chen Chi-tang was dismissed, but Li

Tsung-jen and Pai Tsung-hsi were confirmed in their Kwangsi posts. This was a shrewd step to take since it did not offend Chinese patriotic sentiment: no one would mourn the passing of Chen, while Li and Pai, who commanded wide respect, were not touched. The conference rejected the Southwestern proposal that an anti-Japanese expedition be launched at once. Replying to this motion, Chiang Kai-shek declared that Nanking considered the maintenance of China's territorial integrity the vital point upon which resistance should hinge. He pledged that China would not sign any treaty detrimental to its territorial integrity and would fight rather than recognize Manchoukuo. Yet, the hope for peace was not gone, he said, and the past six months had even offered greater promise in this respect.

Not only did Nanking now have effective control of Kwangtung, but by early September the Kwangsi affair was practically over. Li Tsung-jen was to remain in the province as Pacification Commissioner, and Pai Tsung-hsi was to become a member of the Standing Committee of the Military Affairs Commission in the national capital. In a statement to the country they declared that Nanking had accepted in full Kwangsi's views on national salvation. Before long it was agreed that the Kwangsi troops should come under Nanking's nominal control as the Fifth Route Army, with the Central government bearing a major share of the expenses. Nanking emerged from the crisis more than ever the symbol of China's national power. But it must not be forgotten that the participants in the settlement were swayed by the rising patriotic feelings of the Chinese people, who were not in a mood to tolerate internal squabbling or new outbreaks of civil conflict.

In December 1936, however, a far more dangerous situation arose when Chiang Kai-shek was seized by his own troops at Sian in the Northwest. Chang Hsueh-liang, former Manchurian warlord who had lost his territory to Japan in 1931, was the leading figure in this incident. Though deeply loyal to Chiang, he had entertained doubts about policy for some time. In the fall of 1935 he suffered a severe defeat in anti-Communist operations, and two of his divisions deserted. Gradually a truce was established between the Communists and Chang's Tungpei (i.e., Northeastern, or Manchurian) forces. The latter wished to return to their Manchurian homeland and had no heart for fighting their fellow-Chinese. Moreover, they were not being paid regularly and received no reinforcements. In June 1936 Chang Hsueh-liang met Chou En-lai, the Communist leader, for the first time, and by autumn Sian had become an anti-Japanese center.

The Communists were now accelerating their drive for a national united front. On August 25, 1936 they once more appealed to the Kuomintang to end civil war and begin resistance. It was asserted that if a democratic republic was established in China, the Soviet regions would become a part of it, would send delegates to participate in the National Assembly and would establish in their own territory a democratic system similar to that introduced in the rest of the country. Soon afterward informal Nanking-Communist discussions took place. The government was now adopting a firmer tone in dealing with the Japanese, but at the same time sought to hold the movement for resistance in check. A complicated effort was being made to avoid immediate resistance, to modify official policies sufficiently to satisfy an angry public opinion, and to prevent opposition elements from growing stronger.

The official position, as privately urged, was that China was not ready to resist Japan, would need considerable time to prepare for resistance, and therefore should not take any action that might provoke Tokyo to launch an attack. The reply of the National Salvationists, Communists and others was that Japanese aggression would continue and even be encouraged by Chinese "good behavior," that the longer resistance was postponed the more success Japan would have in swallowing China piece-meal, and that if the government planned to resist it should bring civil war to a halt. The official rejoinder was that only the defeat of the Communists or their submission to Central authority could lay the basis for national unity. The opposing points of view were expressed in the slogans, "Unity through resistance" and "Unity before resistance," which meant very different things in practice, even though in pure logic they might not appear to be far apart.

The confused tendencies of the time are revealed in the record. On October 12 the Central government endorsed a strongly-worded patriotic manifesto issued by sixty-six leading Peiping intellectuals. Chiang Kai-shek began to use the term, "national salvation," and held a series of conferences with military leaders to discuss Japanese threats in North China. He next visited Sian and Loyang where he opposed the truce between Chang Hsueh-liang and the Communists. In November, while conversations were going on between the Chinese and Japanese Foreign Ministers, Japan used puppet Mongolian and Manchurian troops for an invasion of Suiyuan province in the north. At once there was a united national demand for resistance in a movement that stretched from Peiping to Canton and embraced businessmen and radicals alike. But Nanking gave little aid to the Suiyuan forces, which were nevertheless able to repel the invaders. Meanwhile three Central divisions belonging to General Hu Tsung-nan's crack First Army attacked the Communists in Kansu and were badly beaten.

Earlier an important strike had broken out among Shanghai cotton mill workers. Not only did it soon become concentrated in the Japanese mills and assume an openly political character, but it spread quickly to the northern cities of Tientsin, Tsingtao and Tsinan, receiving the support of the Shanghai National Salvation bodies which were being backed publicly by merchants and bankers in that center. In order to break the strike—the first significant act of Chinese labor in some years—Japan landed forces at Tsingtao and later raided Kuomintang offices there. Yet, in the midst of these new instances of Japanese aggression, seven outstanding National Salvation leaders were arrested in Shanghai on a charge of committing treasonable, subversive acts. Since Japan had declared that the National Salvation Association was responsible for the mill strikes, these arrests were particularly disturbing to patriotic groups.

Early in December Chiang Kai-shek visited Sian again. Previously, in Loyang, he had rejected Chang Hsueh-liang's personal request that at least part of the troops in the Northwest be sent to the Suiyuan front, but had promised to go to Sian to explain matters to the Tungpei commanders. Chiang now found that he could not win them over to the idea of renewed anti-Communist operations, for their only wish was to resist Japan. On December 10 he declared that if Chang Hsueh-liang and his army refused to obey, they would be transferred south. On the following day, at a meeting of Chang Hsueh-liang and other Tungpei military men, the decision was reached to arrest Chiang and his staff. Chang Hsueh-liang issued strict orders that he be taken alive. On December 12, 1936 the Generalissimo was seized.

The Sian leaders attacked Nanking's policy of non-resistance in a public statement and put forward the following program:

"1. Reorganize the Nanking Government, and admit all parties to share the joint responsibility of saving the nation.
"2. Stop all kinds of civil wars.
"3. Immediately release the patriotic leaders arrested in Shanghai.
"4. Release all political prisoners throughout the country.
"5. Emancipate the patriotic movement of the people.
"6. Safeguard the political freedom of the people to organize and call meetings.
"7. Actually carry out the Will of Dr. Sun Yat-sen.
"8. Immediately call a National Salvation Conference."[5]

Opinion in the Northwest was divided as to the next move. Chang Hsueh-liang and many others still considered Chiang their leader. Their object was simply to effect his "awakening" and then allow him to return to Nanking to carry out new policies. On the other hand, some of the Tungpei radicals, deeply disillusioned with Nanking, wished to kill Chiang. The balance of power was held by the Communists, who had played no part whatever in the seizure of the Generalissimo and, after that event, were the group most anxious for Chiang's release and peace with Nanking. The Communists had been working for a long time to reach an agreement with the Central government and were convinced that they were on the road to success. Understanding as they did the necessity of unity if China was to resist Japan, they rejected the possibility of forming an anti-Nanking coalition with the groups in the Northwest.

Immediately after Chiang's seizure, Chang Hsueh-liang sent a plane to bring to Sian Chinese Soviet representatives, who were invited to participate officially in the negotiations and organizational activity in that city. A small Communist delegation, including Chou En-lai, Political Commissar of the First Front Red Army, Yeh Chien-ying, Chief of Staff of the Red East Front Army, and a few others, arrived. Every day Chiang Kai-shek was visited by Chang Hsueh-liang. Chou En-lai and Yeh Chien-ying also saw him. Chou informed Chiang that the Communists were willing to change the name of the Red Army, make the Soviet area a special district of the Chinese Republic, and give pledges against agrarian and social revolution in return for assurances from Nanking.

[5] For full text, see Appendix, pp. 94-95.

The desire of the Communists to effect Chiang's release contrasted strangely with the attitude of some of his associates at Nanking. A temporary administration was established, in which War Minister Ho Ying-chin was placed in charge of troop movements. The key question was whether the regime should initiate negotiations for Chiang's release or use military force against the Northwest. The former move was quite feasible, since Chang Hsueh-liang had asked for discussions, but the Nanking authorities decided that the prestige of the State was more important than the life of one man—even if that man was the only one capable of leading a united China. Hostilities actually took place, but a message received from the Generalissimo at almost the last moment helped to avert the launching of a general punitive expedition. Why some elements at Nanking should have been willing to risk splitting the country wide open was later suggested by a Shanghai publication in these words: "The detention of the Generalissimo . . . was immediately hailed by a certain group or groups in Nanking as a God-given opportunity for seizing the powers which would be relinquished on General Chiang Kai-shek's death, thus bringing to completion plans which had been shaped under cover of a specious loyalty to him."[6] The nature of these elements is suggested by the fact that following Chiang's detention, Ho-Ying-chin invited Wang Ching-wei to return from Europe to China.

The crisis soon reached a partial solution with the return of the Generalissimo to Nanking on December 25. It is clear that when he left Sian, accompanied by his former captor, Chang Hsueh-liang, he had made no written pledge to follow a new policy. Yet, he had very likely indicated orally a change in views. As for Chang, he understood that, if civil war was to be avoided, he would have to release the Generalissimo and gamble on the permanence of this change. The Tungpei radicals wished to kill Chiang, but the Communists managed to shake their determination, even though failing actually to convince most of them.

Sian was a cross-section of Chinese politics. It indicated the irrepressibility of the popular desire for national resistance and the cessation of civil war. It showed clearly that Nanking would have to change its course, if it was to retain moral leadership of the nation. And it suggested that in the absence of opportunities for free, public discussion of national affairs the popular

[6] *North-China Herald* (Shanghai), January 13, 1937.

movement might express itself in undesirable ways. The crisis also revealed unsuspected antagonisms within the Nanking regime and proved how deep was the desire of the Communists for an agreement with the Central Government. Not least significant was the fact that Chiang Kai-shek became the symbol of a new sense of national unity. His release and the avoidance of civil war caused a wave of thankfulness to sweep over the whole of China.

Yet, the possibility of conflict in the Northwest continued after Sian, for Chiang's return did not settle the problem of military and political power in that area. Indeed, during January and early February 1937, it was only by a narrow margin that armed clashes were avoided. But the meeting of the Kuomintang Central Executive Committee in mid-February indicated that internal issues were being resolved in favor of resistance to the foreign aggressor. The first open sign of a new current of thought in Nanking circles took the form of a joint statement by fourteen members of the Kuomintang and the government —including Feng Yu-hsiang, Sun Fo and Mme. Sun Yat-sen— urging a return to Sun Yat-sen's policies of cooperation with the Communists and the U.S.S.R.

The session also received a telegram from the Chinese Communists suggesting that it adopt the following program: cessation of civil war and concentration of strength against aggression; freedom of speech and assembly, and release of political prisoners; calling of a National Salvation conference representing all groups and armed forces; hastening of preparations for armed resistance; and improvement of the living conditions of the people. If these points were approved, the Communists expressed willingness to cease all armed activity directed toward the overthrow of the National Government; to change the names of the Soviet Government and the Red Army, with both coming under national authority; to establish democratic government in their territory; and to end land confiscation and carry out the national program of resistance. The Central Executive Committee replied by setting four conditions for rapprochement: abolition of the Red Army and its incorporation in the national forces; dissolution of the Soviet Government; cessation of Communist propaganda; and termination of the class struggle. Although the Central Executive Committee's manifesto spoke bitterly of the necessity of "rooting up the red plague," moves toward unity were actually being made.

This was not generally known during the months that followed, and China appeared to be subject to the same confusion of conflicting tendencies that marked the pre-Sian period. Although the general spirit of unity continued to grow, efforts were still being made to reach a settlement with Japan. Privately, however, Kuomintang-Communist negotiations were going forward. After the Sian incident was over Chou En-lai visited Chiang Kai-shek, and Nanking delegates were sent to the Soviet area. The Communists began to carry out the proposals they had made to the Central Executive Committee, and the Central Government showed its desire for harmony by not undertaking a renewal of hostilities in the Northwest. In addition, food and supplies were sent to the Red forces, and agreement was reached that Communist delegates would be included in the National Congress, which was scheduled to meet in November 1937 for the purpose of adopting a constitution. It was expected that in mid-July a public announcement of reconciliation would be issued.

The Japanese attack on July 7 preceded the time set for this declaration and, in effect, settled the question of internal unity. Some circles in Nanking, however, were able to postpone the main statements of agreement until the latter part of September, although it was clear beforehand that unity had been achieved. At the same time there was an unprecedented drawing together of previously hostile elements within China, in the spirit of Chiang Kai-shek's exhortation to the armed forces at the end of July 1937:

"We are all descendants of Huang Ti who have sworn allegiance to the Revolution. Should we not fight to the last and so pay our country what we owe her? Only thus can we be worthy of our great leader, Dr. Sun Yat-sen, and of the heroes who have laid down their lives before us. Only thus can we preserve the spacious land and glorious heritage passed down to us by our ancestors. Only thus can we requite our parents and teachers for the faithful instruction and the training that they have given us. Only thus can we be true to the generations that follow us.

"Soldiers! The supreme moment has come. With one heart and purpose advance. Refuse to retreat. Drive out the unspeakably evil invaders and bring about the rebirth of our nation."[7]

[7]Chiang Kai-shek, *Resistance and Reconstruction* (New York, Harper, 1943), p. 19.

CHAPTER II

UNITY AND RESISTANCE

Nature of the New Unity

The new unity forged in 1937 has proved to be fundamentally stronger than that of the first united front in 1924-27. This is indicated by its continuance, despite many severe strains, through more than seven years of Chinese resistance; while in the twenties unity was shattered after less than half that time. The nature of internal cooperation since 1937 has also been significantly different, for it has rested on a union of virtually the whole people against a foreign aggressor rather than of one part of the country against another. In short, the fact that the present war is international, not civil, suggests the magnitude of China's national growth since 1927. Moreover, the feeling of national unity was far stronger in 1937 than a decade before, not only because of developments during the intervening years, but because of the increasing realization that without unity and resistance China could not survive. The break-up of unity today —as at any time since 1937—would allow the national government no alternative other than to become a Japanese puppet regime. This is in marked contrast to 1927 when, despite the disruption of Kuomintang-Communist cooperation, the Kuomintang was able to establish a functioning Chinese government at Nanking.

It is also important to note that the component groups in the present situation are stronger than they were in the first period of unity—a factor which makes for greater total strength as long as civil war is not renewed. Not least significant, in 1924-27 the Chinese nationalists received outside aid only from the U.S.S.R. and found the other powers hostile to them whereas since 1937 international conditions have been far more favorable to the preservation of Chinese unity, because China's resistance has coincided with the temporary or continuing interests of a large group of foreign countries. Not only has China received aid from the U.S.S.R.—particularly in the period from 1937 to the outbreak of the Soviet-German war —but the United States and Britain even during their appeasement of Japan extended some material help as well as moral support. In the early phase of the war Germany, although a partner of Japan, also furnished military advice and supplies. Today, with China in the ranks of the United Nations, the outside forces making for continued internal agreement are of considerable strength even though there can be no certainty that they will be decisive in all circumstances.

On the other hand, there have been important factors over a period of years that have prevented unity from rising markedly above the minimum level necessary for resistance. Perhaps the outstanding difficulty is that the differences between the Kuomintang and the Communists were greater in 1937 than in 1924, for at the earlier date both groups were in the position of aspiring to power rather than deciding how to use it. The Kuomintang was then a body that had turned to the Soviet Union for aid in its reorganization, so that it could establish a national government and overcome the problems that had beset it since the fall of the Manchus. The Communist Party, only three years old, was weak in numbers and was not regarded at the beginning as a great competitor. Besides, it was the only important internal ally the Kuomintang could hope to have in the struggle against opposing military and political forces in China. In 1937, however, the two parties had behind them ten years of civil war—years that represent an exceptionally sanguinary chapter even in the history of internecine conflict.

As a result of these circumstances, unity was achieved in 1937 only under the unrelenting pressure of a foreign foe and was not sealed with a genuine, formal agreement. In 1924 the Communists, while retaining their own organization, had been admitted in a body into the Kuomintang, becoming part of its membership. Subsequent measures of the Kuomintang had therefore been joint actions. But in 1937 no union of this type took place. Moreover, the cementing of unity was effected through parallel statements, not a single declaration.

Thus, the Communists on September 22, 1937 announced from their capital at Yenan that they had, "on the basis of peace and national unity and joint resistance against foreign aggression, reached an understanding with the Kuomintang."[1] They then proposed the following objectives:

"(1) Struggle for the independence, liberty and emancipation of the Chinese nation by promptly and swiftly preparing and launching the national revolutionary campaign of resistance with a view to recovering the lost territories and restoring the integrity of territorial sovereign rights.

"(2) Enforce democracy based on the people's rights and convoke the National People's Congress in order to enact the Constitution and decide upon the plans of national salvation.

"(3) Improve the well-being and enrich the livelihood of the Chinese people by relieving famines and other calamities, stabilizing the people's livelihood, consolidating national defense and economy, removing the sufferings of the people and bettering their living conditions."

Expressing the belief that the whole country would support these objectives, the manifesto declared:

"The Communist Party of China fully realizes that this programme is likely to meet with numerous difficulties. The first obstacle will come from Japanese Imperialism. In order to deprive the enemy of all pretext for aggression and dispel doubts on the part of friends, the Central Executive Committee of the Communist Party of China solemnly declares the following in connection with national emancipation:

"(1) The San Min Chu-I enunciated by Dr. Sun Yat-sen is the paramount need of China today. This Party is ready to strive for its enforcement.

"(2) This Party abandons its policy of overthrowing the Kuomintang of China by force and the movement of sovietization, and discontinues its policy of forcible confiscation of land from landowners.

"(3) This Party abolishes the present Soviet Government and will enforce democracy based on the people's rights in order to unify the national political machinery.

"(4) This Party abolishes the Red Army, reorganizes it into the National Revolutionary Army, places it under the direct control of the Military Affairs Commission of the National Government, and awaits orders for mobilization to share the responsibility of resisting foreign invasion at the front."

On September 23 Generalissimo Chiang Kai-shek welcomed this manifesto and commented on it. Declaring that "not all of our countrymen have had a sincere and unwavering faith in

[1] For full text, see Appendix, pp. 96-97. Originally drafted by the Communists on July 5, it was handed to the Kuomintang on July 15; but publication was not permitted until September 22. The delay in publication was greatly regretted by Mao Tse-tung.

the Three Principles of the People, nor have they fully realized the magnitude of the crisis confronting the country," he made the following statement:[2]

"During the past few years the National Government has been calling ceaselessly upon the nation to achieve genuine internal solidarity, and to face unitedly the national crisis. Those who have in the past doubted the Three Principles of the People have now realized the paramount importance of our national interests, and have buried their differences for the sake of internal unity. The Chinese people today fully realize that they must survive together or perish together, and that the interests of the nation must take precedence over the interests of individuals or groups.

"The Manifesto recently issued by the Chinese Communist Party is an outstanding instance of the triumph of national sentiment over every other consideration. The various decisions embodied in the Manifesto, such as the abandonment of a policy of violence, the cessation of Communist propaganda, the abolition of the Chinese Soviet Government, and the disbandment of the Red Army are all essential conditions for mobilizing our national strength in order that we may meet the menace from without and guarantee our own national existence.

"These decisions agree with the spirit of the Manifesto and resolutions adopted by the Third Plenary Session of the Kuomintang. The Communist Party's Manifesto declares that the Chinese Communists are willing to strive to carry out the Three Principles. This is ample proof that China today has only one objective in its war efforts . . . :

"If a citizen believes in the Three Principles and works actively for the salvation of the state, the Government should not concern itself with his past, but should give him opportunity to prove his loyalty in service to the Republic. Likewise, the Government will gladly accept the services of any political organization provided it is sincerely working for the nation's salvation, and is willing under the banner of our national revolution to join with us in our struggle against aggression.

"The Chinese Communist Party, by surrendering its prejudices, has clearly recognized the vital importance of our national independence and welfare. I sincerely hope that all members of the Communist Party will faithfully and unitedly put into practice the various decisions reached, and under the unified military command that is directing our resistance, will offer their services to the state, fighting shoulder to shoulder with the rest of the nation for the successful completion of the Nationalist Revolution."

Although the new unity was launched under the unfavorable auspices of a decade of civil war, internal harmony was at a

---

[2] For full text of this statement, see Appendix, pp. 98-99.

high level during the period of more than a year between July 1937 and the fall of Hankow at the end of October 1938. The constant fighting of these months, the necessity for the utmost cooperation in defending a wide front, the spirit of solidarity engendered by the cessation of Chinese appeasement of Japan —all these developments forced political differences into the background and brought the points of agreement to the fore. In the north the Eighth Route Army (formerly the Chinese Red Army), with official approval, began to reorganize areas in the rear of the Japanese for guerrilla warfare on the basis of a program of social, economic, and political reform. Some time afterward former Communist partisan troops were reorganized into the New Fourth Army for the purpose of operating behind the Japanese lines in the lower Yangtze valley. Within the national government and the Kuomintang, defeatists like Wang Ching-wei were obliged to retreat and, although still able to exert much influence, could no longer dominate policy. The government service itself began to take in small numbers of liberals and radicals who had previously been excluded. This was indicated not only by the appointment of Chou En-lai as Vice Director of the Political Training Board of the National Military Council, but also by the employment in administrative posts of various National Salvationists and liberal patriots. At the same time, despite certain exceptions, there was a new freedom of speech and press, with opportunities for expression in conversation and print that had not existed for many years. One indication of this was the considerable expansion of the Life bookshops which published and sold innumerable pamphlets, books and magazines of a liberal character. Another was the establishment in Hankow of a Communist newspaper, the *Hsin Hua Jih Pao* (New China Daily), at the beginning of 1938 with the permission of the government and an initial monetary contribution from Finance Minister H. H. Kung.

Throughout 1937 and 1938 the government became increasingly forthright in statements and actions favoring continued resistance. At first, few if any of the Kuomintang leaders had believed that the country could fight very long. Their hope was that if China resisted Japan for a period—perhaps six months, or a year at most—Tokyo would moderate its demands and be willing to consider peace through third-power intervention. That a war to the end was not at first envisaged is indicated not

only by the statements of many high officials, but also by the fact
that not until early in 1938 was the Chinese Minister withdrawn
from Japan. Moreover, in the late autumn of 1937, especially
as the capture of Nanking drew near, the Germans attempted
mediation of the conflict. At every point, however, the tempta-
tion to conclude peace was rejected by dominant circles within
the regime, partly because of the temper of the people, partly
because it was patent that, in the last analysis, peace could mean
nothing but submission to Japan. Finally, in December 1938,
the defection of Wang Ching-wei to the Japanese side indicated
that the forces of resistance had met the supreme test. Despite
the loss of the main cities, it had been decided that China would
continue the struggle and undertake a prolonged war.[3]

One of the high points of Chinese political progress during
this early stage of resistance was the convening of an Extraordinary Congress of Kuomintang Delegates at the end of
March 1938. This emergency session of the Kuomintang decided
on the establishment of the People's Political Council (see pp.
50-53). It also adopted a forward-looking statement of policy
covering the main aspects of the war effort. The nature of this
Program of Resistance and Reconstruction, as it was called, can
be gathered from the following sections:

2. All war-time powers and forces are hereby placed under the
   control of the Kuomintang and of General Chiang Kai-shek.
8. The army shall receive more political training, so that both
   officers and men may appreciate the importance of war-time
   national reconstruction and be ready to lay down their lives
   for the nation.
10. All people who have arms of their own shall receive the
    support and encouragement of the Government and, under
    the direction of local military authorities, shall cooperate
    with the regular army to defend the country against foreign
    invasion. Guerrilla warfare shall be waged in the enemy's
    rear with the object of smashing and dividing his military
    forces.
14. A thorough reform in the central and local governmental
    machinery shall be instituted with the object of simplifying
    and making it rational. Only thus can administrative effi-
    ciency be obtained to meet the urgent needs of war.

[3] Japanese peace feelers have continued throughout the war. Some elements in
Chungking were at various points apparently willing to consider a "negotiated
peace" with Tokyo, mainly at times of Japanese military successes or Axis victories in Europe.

16. Corrupt officials shall be severely punished, and their property shall be confiscated.
17. Economic reconstruction shall concern itself mainly with matters of military importance, and incidentally with matters that contribute to the improvement of the livelihood of the people . . .
26. In the course of the war, the freedom of speech, the freedom of the press, and the freedom of assembly shall be fully guaranteed to the people, provided they do not contravene Dr. Sun Yat-sen's revolutionary principles or the provisions of the law.[4]

Guerrilla Warfare and Prolonged Resistance

Since China was considerably weaker than Japan both economically and politically, it had to develop methods of warfare that would permit the most effective use of its sources of strength —notably the size of its population, the extent of its territory, the patriotic spirit of its people, and the support that would probably come from foreign powers over a period of years. A protracted war was required to take advantage of these circumstances, since a brief decisive conflict would inevitably mean the victory of the stronger party, Japan. But the war could be prolonged only if China was willing to yield its most important eastern centers and devote its energies to building up the undeveloped interior, while waging a guerrilla struggle in the Japanese rear and attacking the enemy with mobile, regular forces at the front. Positional fighting would, of course, take place; but in general the Chinese, because of their inferior equipment and training, would have to avoid all-out contests for fixed points.

Although mobile and guerrilla warfare are military concepts, they have far-reaching social implications. To give up the idea of fighting for positions meant that the government would have to resolve to continue resistance despite the loss of the coastal regions from which its chief economic and political support had come. This would also prove a severe test of the loyalty of the landowners and powerful urban interests in the invaded areas, whose properties would come under Japanese rule. Moreover, to engage in guerrilla warfare, it would be necessary to mobilize the people behind the Japanese lines by offering them improvements in their way of life. The peasants could hardly

[4] For full text, see Appendix, pp. 100-103.

develop the initiative necessary for guerrilla activity or be willing to accept the risks involved, if no amelioration of their
economic and political position took place. But to make such
changes would be to transform the Chinese countryside and
greatly reduce the power of the landlords.

The Communists were the first to suggest a strategy of prolonged war. But there were others—for example, the Kwangsi
generals, Pai Tsung-hsi and Li Tsung-jen, who reached similar
conclusions on military policy. Indeed, early in the war Li
organized guerrilla and mobile fighting in the Anhui-Kiangsu-
Shantung area. The larger part of guerrilla resistance, however,
has been carried on by the Eighth Route Army and associated
forces rather than by the troops of the Central government.
Dispatched to Shansi province in 1937 under orders of the
Central authorities, the Eighth Route Army found burnt and
empty villages, pro-Japanese Peace Maintenance Committees
and general demoralization, but it gave direction to existing
spontaneous guerrilla groups and revived local morale and
administration. Popular organizations were established; a guerrilla force was formed to attack communications and small
groups of Japanese soldiers; and an unarmed Self-Defense Corps
was raised to patrol roads, carry information and help care for
the wounded. The people received patriotic instruction through
schools, plays, speeches, songs, and wall newspapers. Economic
difficulties were alleviated, but at the same time every effort was
made to moderate class friction. The army received daily political and cultural education; simple, friendly relations existed
between officers and men; and emphasis was placed on the
importance of respecting the rights of the people.

The nature of guerrilla policy can be seen more concretely
from reports of developments in Central Hopei, one of the
subdivisions of the Hopei-Shansi-Chahar Border Government,
which was established in January 1938. Before many months
had passed, 15% of the agricultural land in Central Hopei had
been redistributed through confiscation of the property of
traitors, division of public lands, and allotment of land whose
owners fled after the invasion. Rents were cut 25 per cent, the
eviction of tenants was prohibited, a three-year moratorium
was established on all debts, the maximum legal interest rate
was set at 10 per cent annually, and the old burdensome land
tax was reformed on a graduated basis, with over one-fourth

of the poorest peasants exempt. In order to increase the food supply and to prevent Japan from using the area's resources, the cotton crop was cut by 70 per cent in 1938 and wheat was grown instead. Local handicrafts were encouraged with the object of reducing purchases from Japanese-controlled territory to a minimum. Significantly, despite the agrarian reforms, a number of former wealthy citizens returned from the towns to which they had fled, apparently finding the policy adopted in Central Hopei a comparatively reasonable one.[5]

As a result of guerrilla activities in the north, the Japanese suffered serious casualties and saw an important part of their plans for the conquest of China disrupted. To this day, although Japan controls the main communications lines in the invaded areas, it has not succeeded in taking over the countryside as a whole. In consequence, it has not been able to exploit China as it intended, while the patriotic spirit of the people in many areas cut off from Chungking has been kept high. These factors have been of the utmost significance in China's continued resistance.

Wang Ching-wei and the Peace Party

It is indicative of China's unity that very few officials have gone over to the enemy, and that only one of these—Wang Ching-wei—has been a figure of national significance. This is all the more striking because in political outlook Wang was not far apart from many other leaders who remained in Chungking and continued to participate in the war of resistance. Thus, if he was opposed to Chiang Kai-shek, it was also true that at the time of Sian similar elements in Nanking had almost sacrificed Chiang's life by their intransigent attitude toward the northern rebels. If he was in favor of appeasing Japan, certainly there were others both before and after July 1937 who held a similar point of view. Nor was his strong opposition to the Communists and the popular patriotic movement in any way peculiar to himself. What was distinctive in Wang was a special personal factor that led him to go over to the enemy instead of continuing to promote his treacherous views within Chungking itself.

[5] This and the previous paragraph have been adapted from the author's article, "Politics and Strategy of China's Mobile War," *Pacific Affairs* (New York), September 1939, pp. 267, 270. Since 1938 the details of guerrilla practice have changed in accordance with circumstances, but the program remains fundamentally the same.

The characteristic elements entering into Wang's actions were his inordinate ambition, and his lack of any means of satisfying this lust for power. Although he had been, at least in theory, the second most important personality within the government, in practice he had neither armed forces nor a great popular following behind him. Consequently, despite the fact that he was considered a brilliant orator and was known throughout the country, in any decisive showdown he wielded less influence than many relatively minor figures who had troops at their disposal and were not obsessed by the desire for supreme power. This lack of internal backing explains why, time after time, he was defeated in attempts to wrest control of the nationalist movement from Chiang Kai-shek. It also lies behind his turning to foreign powers, for his reliance on Japan and Germany was in large part an effort to compensate for lack of support at home. This has been characteristic of traitors in all times and places.

A less ambitious man who possessed armed support or a reasonably secure place in the Kuomintang organization would have trimmed his sails to the prevailing political winds. Wang, however, apparently felt that he had thoroughly committed himself to one line of policy and that it had to be all or nothing. This was particularly true in connection with the issue of Chinese resistance. Once it became clear that, despite the fall of the leading centers, the country would continue to fight, his only hope lay in trying to end the war by going over to the enemy. To stay within Chungking meant that, while he might retain posts of great nominal importance, he would, in fact, be displaced more and more by other, shrewder persons who had not burned their political bridges behind them.

As long as he remained in Free China, Wang was a focal point for the elements opposed to resistance. In December 1937, for example, after German efforts to mediate the Far Eastern war had begun, he suggested the desirability of peace in a special interview in Hankow. Early in 1938, in an illuminating declaration entitled, "Guerrilla Warfare and the Scorched Earth," he condemned subtly but unmistakably all efforts to mobilize the people politically and asserted that no propaganda for resistance was necessary, since "except for a few traitors here and there every Chinese man, woman and child realizes the necessity of offering resistance against aggression and invaders."[6] In the People's Political Council, of which he was elected Speaker at the first session in July 1938, he and his supporters made every effort to promote peace sentiment, but were unsuccessful in winning over the members. As the fall of Hankow drew near, Wang declared that, if Japan offered peace terms which did not hamper the existence of the Chinese nation, such proposals might serve as a basis for discussion. In December he privately urged the Generalissimo to use a statement previously made by Japanese Premier Konoye as the occasion for peace negotiations. But Chiang refused to follow this suggestion. Shortly after the middle of the month Wang went by airplane to Kunming, the capital of Yunnan, where he made a last effort to strengthen himself by discussing the question of peace with General Lung Yun, the provincial chairman. Unsuccessful in this attempt, he crossed the border into French Indo-China and later went to Nanking to head a puppet regime.

Wang Ching-wei's flight had a two-fold significance. On the one hand, it was a maneuver in the struggle to bring about capitulation to Japan, a new move which indicated that with the fall of Canton and Hankow the war had entered its second phase. In the attrition stage Japan's plans required the establishment of as strong an anti-Chungking political center as possible, one which would be more powerful than the utterly discredited puppet regimes it had previously set up in occupied Nanking and Peiping. It was now necessary for Tokyo to create effective rather than nominal control over the invaded areas. For this some open break in the Chinese national front was required, since the leading economic groups in North China and the lower Yangtze valley still looked to Chungking for guidance, while the mass of the people were influenced directly or in spirit by the guerrilla movement. On the other hand, if Wang's departure was a new blow struck by the appeasers of Japan, it was also a sign that the capitulators in Chungking had been defeated at a moment of supreme significance. The spirit of the people was high, and they were ready for a protracted struggle against Japan.

Although Wang was expelled from the Kuomintang on December 31, 1938, the government moved very slowly in break-

[6] For full text of this declaration, see *The People's Tribune*, Shanghai, June 1938.

ing with him completely. For a while there was hope in some official quarters that he might be induced to return. Japan also moved carefully in committing itself to Wang and did not recognize the regime which he subsequently established at Nanking until November 30, 1940, i.e., almost two years after he first left Chungking, and eight months after the regime was first set up. This points to one of the cardinal facts about Japan's puppet policy: that, although willing to use Wang or any other individual traitor, it realizes that its main objective on the continent—bringing Chinese resistance to an end—could be achieved only through an agreement or understanding with Chungking. Cooperation with Wang has not been an end in itself, but a means of putting pressure on the forces of Chinese resistance. There is every reason to believe that Japan has been willing at all times to sacrifice the puppet regime at Nanking for the sake of a settlement with Chungking. This does not mean, however, that Wang would also be sacrificed, since a government of capitulation might raise no objection to his return—possibly in a more powerful role than before.*

Wang failed in 1938 chiefly because of three factors. First of all, the desire of the Chinese people and many of their leaders —especially Chiang Kai-shek—for unity and resistance made it impossible for wavering politicians to secure acceptance of Japan's terms. Moreover, Japan's offer was so unsatisfactory that no leader who did not wish to become a puppet protected by Japanese bayonets could afford to yield. Finally, foreign aid to China strengthened the determination of the Chinese government. It is not an accident that at three critical points—in December 1938 when Wang deserted, in March 1940 when his regime was established, and in November 1940 when Japan recognized the regime—the United States made loans to Chungking. The American object was to bolster China's resistance.

Rifts in Chinese Unity

Although Chungking rejected Wang's peace proposals, the beginning of the stalemate period in the war was accompanied by the development of friction within China itself. Kuomintang-Communist differences which, even during the Hankow period, had never been wholly absent, now came to the surface again. Moreover, dissension was not limited to the two leading parties, but extended to relations between the Kuomintang and various

* Wang Ching-wei has died (November 1944) since this was written.

minor or weakly organized groups. In the spring of 1938, for example, the government, in effect, dissolved all non-Kuomintang youth organizations by refusing them the necessary official registration. Thus, in Kuomintang territory the student groups that had played so important a role in bringing about resistance were no longer able to function. This fact indicates that, while the most striking instances of friction have occurred between the Kuomintang and the Communists, the official attitude toward other organizations is not markedly different. Nor is hostility confined to liberal groups, for there is ample evidence that conservative minority parties—such as the National Socialist Party, (unconnected with the Nazis except in name), Young China Party, and Vocational Education Group—have also found it difficult to operate under conditions of one-party rule.[7]

While friction may be said, in a general sense, to arise from political differences, the catalyzing elements in the situation are to be found elsewhere—in military conditions, economic difficulties, and China's international position. It is not surprising that friction was at a minimum during the Shanghai-Nanking-Hankow period, when China was engaged in active positional fighting for important centers, and wartime economic problems were still in an early stage of development. Nor is it an accident that later, when Japan was putting comparatively little new military pressure on Chinese forces and when prices were rising to phenomenal levels, political differences appeared in serious form.

China's internal relations are also affected markedly by the attitude of the foreign powers, since the forward-looking groups in the Kuomintang advocate close relations with the western powers, especially the United States, while the reactionary elements, in the main, have opposed such a policy. Anything in the actions of Britain and the United States that serves to discredit these countries in Chinese eyes is used by the latter to advance their own point of view on domestic issues. Thus, the closing of the Burma Road for three months in the summer of 1940 was accompanied by a worsening of the political situation, not simply because the loss of supplies promoted inflation, or because the possibility of China's defeat was increased, but also because those Chinese who had argued for

---

[7] See "Democracy vs. One-Party Rule in Kuomintang China: The 'Little Parties' Organize," *Amerasia* (New York), April 25, 1943. For the text of a manifesto issued by a federation of the small parties, see Appendix, pp. 122-123.

closer cooperation with the Western powers found the ground cut from under their feet. The same thing happened in even more serious form, after Pearl Harbor, when the United States and Britain suffered a great decline in prestige as a result of severe defeats inflicted by the Japanese in Southeast Asia.

The most dangerous outbreak of friction so far occurred early in 1941 when inflation was first becoming a serious political question. Not only does inflation create friction by increasing China's internal problems of livelihood, but it has the specific effect of undermining the prestige of the liberal and westernized groups, consisting in large part of students, teachers, professional men and government employees. These members of the middle class have been hardest hit by the rise in prices and, faced with the problem of maintaining their physical existence, have lost considerably in political influence. This is all the more true because it is only through special government and private allotments of food and other necessities that the intellectuals are able to secure the essentials of living not covered by their incomes. Such a situation plainly does not make for high morale or independence of thought. Moreover, in an effort to curb price increases and regulate production, the government has undertaken many measures of economic control. These policies have not been markedly successful, but they have given rise to a corps of special police, some of which have supplemented other special secret police bodies in curbing liberal sentiment.

The main instances of friction known to the outside world relate, however, to Kuomintang-Communist relations. Even as early as the end of 1938 a military clash occurred in north Honan between Eighth Route Army and Central troops. In 1939, military friction appeared not only in the guerrilla areas, but also on the frontiers of the Border Region in the northwest. Small conflicts which had seemed at first to be isolated incidents, possibly of no national significance, now became symptoms of a general political trend in Chungking. Within certain Kuomintang circles theories developed concerning the desirability of suppressing what were called "alien parties." At the beginning of 1940 serious fighting broke out in Shansi province between forces friendly to the Eighth Route Army and hostile troops. A series of clashes followed in Hopei, Shantung, northern Kiangsu and Anhui, and on the Chekiang-Kiangsu border.

These were accompanied by a worsening of political relations. During the greater part of 1940 discussions went on between the Communists and the Government over a settlement of differences, but the negotiations failed. At the beginning of 1941 Central troops attacked the rearguard of the New Fourth Army and attempted to wipe it out. A section was destroyed, but the bulk of the New Fourth Army continued to operate as a unified guerrilla force despite an order from Chungking for its dissolution.

This incident—one of the low points in Kuomintang-Communist relations—brought China close to what some observers feared would be civil war. The Communists refused to attend the session of the People's Political Council in March 1941 unless the Central authorities complied with a series of demands, including the cessation of anti-Communist moves, reparation for the action against the New Fourth Army, the punishment of persons responsible (including Ho Ying-chin, the Minister of War), and the adoption of new policies by the Central government. Chiang Kai-shek rejected these demands and gave the Central view of the situation in an address of March 6, 1941 to the People's Political Council. Presenting the official explanation of the attack on the New Fourth Army, he declared that the Communists, in effect, were asking the Central government not to "suppress disobedient and rebellious troops." He suggested that the Communists had not kept their pledges to the government, but stated with reference to fears of civil war, that "at no future time could there conceivably be another campaign for the suppression of the Communists."[8]

Since 1941 there has been comparatively little military friction, but Kuomintang-Communist relations have not improved. Indeed, in the summer of 1943 there were rumors that the Central authorities were planning to attack the Border Region and that, for this purpose, new divisions had been sent to the Northwest to join Chungking troops regularly stationed there against the Communists.[9] When the Kuomintang Central

[8] Chiang Kai-shek, *Resistance and Reconstruction*, cited, p. 240. For full text of this address, see Appendix, pp. 115-121. For the Communist view of the New Fourth Army incident, see Appendix, pp. 111-114.

[9] For comment on the situation at this time, see Lawrence K. Rosinger, "Explosive Conditions in China Worry United Nations," *Foreign Policy Bulletin* (New York), August 13, 1943, and "Kuomintang-Communist Friction Hampers China's Resistance," *ibid.*, September 3, 1943.

Executive Committee met in September 1943, it was reported to have received a statement from the Shantung provincial government on a clash between Communist troops and the provincial Peace Preservation Corps. At a subsequent session, Chiang Kai-shek gave the Committee "instructions for the settlement" of the Kuomintang-Communist problem.

". . . we should clearly recognize," he said, "that the Chinese Communist problem is a purely political problem and should be solved by political means. . . . you should maintain the policy of leniency and forbearance which we have consistently pursued in dealing with our domestic affairs with the expectation that the Chinese Communist Party will be moved by our sincerity and magnanimity no matter in what way they may slander us nor in what manner they may try to create trouble." He declared that the Communists would once more be treated "with sympathy and consideration," if they met the government's demands.[10] There was no indication, however, that this represented a fundamental change in government policy. In fact, the resolution subsequently passed by the Committee contained no reference to the use of "political means" alone in dealing with the Communists, but spoke instead of persuading them "in an appropriate manner" to do what was desired of them.[11]

Subsequently, in a resolution of September 27, the People's Political Council attacked the Communists sharply. But on October 20, in his first press conference, the new Minister of Information, Liang Han-tsao, declared that "no such thing as a clash is impending between the Kuomintang and the Communists." He told reporters that the current Communist attitude toward the Central government was "moderate." On the previous day, the Generalissimo had appointed a committee of fifty-three, including two Communists, to lay the groundwork for constitutional government. It was noted by foreign observers, however, that Minister Liang's statement was not published by any Chinese language newspaper in Chungking. Nor was it contained in the Chinese language reports of the official Central News Agency. When questioned on this point, the Minister stated on October 27 that it was not necessary "to educate the Chinese people by saying that there will be no civil war," but

10 For full text of Chiang's statement, see Appendix, pp. 124-125.
11 For full text of the Central Executive Committee's statement, see Appendix, pp. 126-127.

that foreigners "are not so well informed and we must explain to them."[12]

At this time an important external factor was being introduced into the Chinese political situation, namely, the concern of the United States, Britain and Russia that Chinese unity be preserved and strengthened both in the war and postwar periods. The British, perhaps because of anxiety not to put a further burden on relations already strained by the debacle in southeast Asia, tended to avoid public expressions of opinion on the subject. But the Russians showed clearly how they felt in the summer of 1943 when the Moscow publication, *War and the Working Class*, printed a highly critical article warning against the danger of civil war in China and the possibility that a peace agreement might be reached with Japan. In the United States, also, many critical articles were published, and there was good reason to think that the government was concerned about Chinese political conditions. The first suggestion of the use of diplomatic pressure by Washington was found in newspaper reports that at the Cairo conference in November 1943 the Americans and British emphasized to the Chinese the necessity of cementing internal unity for the sake of waging the war against Japan more effectively.

In February 1944 it was revealed in Chungking that the Communists were to send a delegation to the capital. The arrangements took some time, but early in May Lin Tsu-han, Chairman of the Communist-controlled Shensi-Kansu-Ninghsia Border Region, arrived in Sian, where he was met by two Central representatives: Wang Shih-chieh, Secretary-General of the People's Political Council, and General Chang Chih-chung, Minister of the Political Training Board of the National Military Council. The preliminary discussions proved satisfactory, and Lin went to Chungking. He subsequently saw the Generalissimo, and on May 24th it was announced that Chiang had instructed the Central representatives to continue the conversations.

Meanwhile a number of significant internal developments had taken place. In April and May there was a perceptible relaxation of the rigid Chinese censorship, and Chinese liberals were able to speak out more openly than in many years. A group of Chinese and foreign correspondents was also per-

[12] *New York Times*, October 22 and 29, 1943.

mitted to leave on a trip to the Communist areas in the North-west in mid-May—the first break in the official news blockade of the guerrilla regions since 1939. These developments resulted in part from severe foreign criticism of the censorship, especially by correspondents in Chungking, the growing internal economic crisis after almost seven years of war, and the alarmingly rapid advances made by the Japanese in April and May in Honan province, where they seized the important center of Loyang.

There was apparently a general upsurge of criticism of the government in circles thoroughly loyal to it. The most striking instance of this was to be found in speeches delivered by Sun Fo, son of Sun Yat-sen, who is the President of the Legislative Yuan and the leader of the liberal wing of the Kuomintang. Speaking on February 23, 1944 before the Political and Party Affairs Section of the Central Training Institute—the government's school for political instruction of officials—he declared that China could be democratized only if democracy was first realized within the Kuomintang. He pointed out sharply that after sixteen years of political tutelage, there was still "not a single councillor of the *hsien* [district] People's Political Council or a *hsien* administrator elected by the people."[13] And he stated bluntly that "we have come to regard ourselves as if we were the sovereign power entitled to the enjoyment of a special position and to the suppression of all criticism whatsoever against us."[14]

This condition he linked with the attitude of foreign nations toward China and commented on the fact that important organs of opinion in the United States and Britain—such as the *New York Times* and *The Times* of London—had recently shown more sympathy for the Chinese Communists than for the Chungking government. The reaction in these circles, he pointed out, did not result from an interest in Communism, but from fear that the Kuomintang would not carry out democracy. He warned that "if in the postwar era our allies would think that, with the reign of [the] Kuomintang, China would not become a democratic nation, but a fascist and aggressive state, they might take every precaution necessary and would

13 Sun Fo, *China Looks Forward*, (New York, John Day, 1944), p. 111.
14 *Ibid.*, p. 108.

perhaps refuse our co-operation. In that case, China would be isolated."[15]

Sun Fo's remarks were in some respects a reflection of the bitterness of feeling in non-Kuomintang circles in Chungking. In September 1943 Chang Lan, President of the Federation of Chinese Democratic Parties, had issued a statement severely criticizing official policy. Again, in May 1944, the Federation itself declared in a manifesto that it was useless to talk of creating democracy after the war, for if it was not introduced in the course of resistance to Japan the years ahead would be even darker for China than those just past. Words were not spared in lashing out at corruption, the continuance of one-party rule, the denial of civil liberties and the failure to come to grips with China's fundamental problems. The point was also made that criticism from abroad should be accepted as a means toward self-improvement.[16]

The concern of China's allies about conditions in that country was revealed in the summer of 1944 when Vice-President Henry A. Wallace of the United States made a trip to China and Siberia. Mr. Wallace arrived in China on June 20 and left early in July. From the nature of his public statements it was clear that he had the following minimum objectives in mind: to promote better relations between China and Russia, and to encourage China to take steps to avert a future civil war. He also showed a deep interest in China's postwar economic development and the creation of the conditions necessary to its becoming a great market for American goods, to its own advantage and that of the United States. His mission had the twofold character of being a tribute to a valued ally and an effort to prevent that ally from following paths detrimental to itself and world cooperation. This was suggested in his radio address of July 9, 1944 after his return to the United States, when he declared that, before committing themselves fully to participation in China's future economic development, American businessmen "want to be certain . . . that there is no foreseeable likelihood of conflict within China or between China and Russia."[17]

It is as yet too early to assess the results of Mr. Wallace's trip.

[15] *Ibid.*, p. 112.

[16] For Chang Lan's statement, see: "China Needs True Democracy," *Asia and the Americas* (New York), May 1944. The manifesto of May 1944 will be found in the September 1944 issue of *Pacific Affairs*.

[17] *New York Times*, July 10, 1944.

At the present moment the Chinese political situation remains unresolved and, while the possibilities of improvement are brighter than at any time in many years, the necessary government decisions are apparently still to be reached. This was indicated on June 28 when Liang Han-tsao, Minister of Information, asserted that in May, during the campaign in Honan, the Central government had ordered the Communist forces to carry through diversionary actions, but they had neither fought nor replied.[18] Since this was a charge that had frequently been made against the Communists at times of acute friction, its repetition in the midst of political discussions did not seem a hopeful sign. More light was thrown on the difficult aspects of the situation on July 1, when Chou En-lai declared in an interview in Yenan: "There still is considerable distance between the Government's proposals and our suggestions. The Central Committee of our party is considering its reply to these proposals, hoping that a rational solution will be found." A "rational solution" he defined as one "beneficial to unity in the war of resistance and to the promotion of democracy."[19] On July 26 Liang Han-tsao confirmed the existence of a number of differences, but expressed confidence that an agreement would finally be reached.

[18] *Ibid.*, June 29, 1944.
[19] *Ibid.*, July 9, 1944.

CHAPTER III

CHUNGKING AND POLITICAL CHANGE

Wartime Personnel and Organization

One of the striking characteristics of the National Government is the constancy of its leadership. Perhaps no administration in the world has changed so little with respect to the figures operating it and determining its policies during years of war. A glance at the names of outstanding personalities in Chungking today and in Nanking before July 1937 reveals almost the same individuals, with two exceptions. Wang Ching-wei, who became a Japanese Quisling, no longer holds office, and T. V. Soong, now Foreign Minister, was then out of favor, although he filled the by no means unimportant position of Chairman of the Board of Directors of the Bank of China—a post which he has recently lost to Finance Minister H. H. Kung. It is true that many individuals do not hold the same offices as before the war and that open or subtle changes in their relative influence have occurred, but there is no doubt that to a considerable extent politics has consisted of the reshuffling of a small number of personalities.

Although effective government requires some stability of personnel, this unusual uniformity over a period of years raises questions as to whether Chungking has created adequate machinery for bringing new men into the political arena. Indeed, foreign visitors to China have reported frequently that the government does not make proper use of the talent available in the country and that too many important fields are under nominal direction of a few leaders, while subordinates really carry the burden without being subject to the incentives and restraints arising from public responsibility.

That this is not simply a foreign view was indicated by Mme. Chiang Kai-shek early in the war when she wrote a searching analysis of the shortcomings of Chinese officialdom. Referring to the "seven deadly sins"—self-seeking ("squeeze"), "face," cliquism, defeatism, inaccuracy, lack of self-discipline and evasion of responsibility—she condemned in devastating fashion

45

"the Grand Army of the Paid Unemployable," public servants who are "too incompetent to work," but "not too proud to collect their unearned pay."[1] And on at least one occasion the People's Political Council has suggested the desirability of strengthening government organs through the introduction of new personnel.[2]

The machinery of the National Government, like its personnel, has not altered greatly since 1937. In this connection a Chinese political scientist declares: "In so far as the government proper is concerned, there have been surprisingly few changes. . . . in bold relief the war-time administration differs but little from the pre-war administration."[3] And an American student of Chinese government remarks: "To the Western political scientist, it is amazing that they have carried into the years of catastrophic war a unique, complex constitutional system, treasuring it like an ark of the covenant. This is the five-power system."[4]

The former author states that it is true that "the Military Commission has been much expanded, and the Executive Yuan has also undergone changes. But there have been few innovations altering either the character of any of the existing organs of government, be it the Military Commission, the Executive or any other Yuan, or the State Council itself, or the relationship between these organs."[5] The most significant change in organization has been the creation of a Supreme Council of National Defense—later replaced by a Supreme Committee of National Defense—as a substitute for the Central Political Committee, a Kuomintang body in which the highest power resided before the war. The Supreme Council was established in August 1937, and in November the powers of the Central Political Committee were suspended. The fact that the new body was smaller than the old is alleged to have been the principal reason for the change. There was little difference between them in authority,

[1] May-ling Soong Chiang, *China Shall Rise Again* (Harper, New York, 1941), p. 47.

[2] See p. 57 below.

[3] Tuan-sheng Chien, "War-Time Government in China," *The American Political Science Review* (Menasha, Wisconsin), October 1942, pp. 860, 864.

[4] Paul M. A. Linebarger, *The China of Chiang K'ai-shek: A Political Study* (Boston, World Peace Foundation, 1941), p. 42. This five-power organization has already been described briefly on pp. 9-10 above.

[5] Chien, "War-Time Government in China," *cited* p. 864.

except that the Supreme Council possessed an emergency power of legislation not enjoyed by the Central Political Committee.

In the Supreme Committee, which succeeded the Supreme Council in February 1939, greater powers were given to its President (Chiang Kai-shek). The new body also received authority over departments of the Kuomintang—not merely of the government, as previously—and was empowered to issue orders to subordinate departments of the Military Commission and the Five Yuan instead of having contact only with the head offices of these agencies. Decisions on policy and the initiation and formulation of important measures rest for the most part with the Supreme Committee, particularly its Standing Committee. The establishment of the Supreme Committee was a move toward the further centralization of authority, especially in the hands of the Generalissimo, during the war.[6]

Chiang Kai-shek*

The length of China's war of resistance has caused some of the significant changes that have occurred since 1937 to become indistinct in the public mind. It is not generally appreciated, for example, how greatly Chiang Kai-shek's prestige and formal power have increased during these years. When the pre-war government at Nanking was engaging in civil conflict and yielding ground to Japan, it was not uncommon for Chinese to regard Chiang with hostility or indifference as the latest in a long line of warlords. But after Sian, and especially after the beginning of resistance, he became a genuine symbol of national unity for all patriotic groups and for the mass of the Chinese people. This growth in stature of the Generalissimo, on the basis of his firm will to continue the struggle against Japan, has been one of the major political facts of the war period.

It is difficult to trace in detail the rise of a man's prestige, but the nature of Chiang's governmental position is more easily described. He is the Generalissimo, holds the Presidency of the Military Commission, the Executive Yuan and the Central Executive Committee of the Kuomintang, and was for a time a member of the Presidium of the People's Political Council of which he had previously been the Speaker. He is also the President of the Supreme Committee of National Defense, i.e., the

[6] *Ibid.*, pp. 864-69. Linebarger, *The China of Chiang K'ai-shek*, cited, pp. 46-52.
* See p. 61 for reference to Chiang's more recent position.

key official in the key body within the administration. In the spring of 1938 he was made Director-General of the Kuomintang, a post that had been vacant since the death of Sun Yat-sen thirteen years before. This elevation to the most honored position in the party took the form of Chiang's being named Tsung-tsai, a title almost identical in significance with Sun's designation of Tsung-li. Approximately two and a half years later, on September 13, 1943 he was appointed President of the National Government, succeeding Lin Sen who had died the previous month. This post, which previously had been of a formal character, was now endowed with far-reaching powers.

Though Chiang's position approximates that of a dictator in its apparent scope of authority, actually Chinese economic, political and social conditions are of such a character as to impose important checks on any attempt to establish genuinely centralized control. The technical means—railroads, telephones, radios—are lacking, and the power of the localities remains too great. Nor do the Chinese people show any signs of being inclined toward one-man rule. Moreover, in actual operation, the government is a coalition of many different personal leaders and supporting groups, with the Generalissimo holding the position of supreme leader and coordinator of the various tendencies. The cliques recognize that they cannot get along without him, and he understands that if they are weakened too greatly, the government, as it is now constituted, will be undermined.

Although he throws the weight of his influence now in one direction, now in another, it does not appear that he has ever attempted to destroy any of the constituent groups making up the regime. This is indicated by the fact that, even after Wang Ching-wei left Chungking at the end of 1938, Chiang urged him to return. Such tendencies toward compromise are a reflection not only of traditional Chinese practices, but of the homogeneity of interest felt by China's ruling circles. Consequently, while the Generalissimo in theory can always have his way, in practice he is confronted by sharp limitations on his power. To attempt absolute rule within the government would threaten the break-up of the existing coalition. Besides, Chiang, like any other leader of his importance, is greatly dependent upon the points of view of those who surround and advise him.

The Kuomintang

At this juncture it may be useful to discuss the character of the Kuomintang, without repeating points already made. The Kuomintang is, first of all, the only Chinese political party with legal status. Other groups are non-legal or illegal and exist either by the Kuomintang's sufferance or as a result of its inability to suppress them. Historically, the Kuomintang is the party of China's national revolution. Under Sun Yat-sen, its predecessor, the Tung Meng Hui, played a major part in the revolution of 1911. During 1924-27 it was a national coalition whose chief objective was the unification of China under a single independent regime. After 1927 it was the party of the new Chinese government at Nanking, and in 1937 it was the leader of Chinese resistance against Japan, in association with the Communists and other groups. The history of modern China is clearly inseparable from the history of the Kuomintang and its two leaders, Sun Yat-sen and Chiang Kai-shek.

Much has been written about the groups that make up the Kuomintang, but where personalities play so important a part in politics it is difficult to be certain of detailed facts. Some of the cliques commonly mentioned in discussions of Chinese government are the "C. C.", the Whampoa (or Huangpu) and the Political Science (Cheng Hsueh) groups. It is essential, however, not to conceive of these circles as if they were organized political bodies, holding meetings, passing resolutions and containing enrolled members. Basically any circle or clique is a combination of a leader and his personal following. Most of the cliques, it must be noted, are extremely conservative in outlook.

The problems inherent in this political situation have been indicated by a Chinese writer, already quoted, who declares: "The politically articulate groups outside the Kuomintang have always clamored for democracy, and their voice is likely to be louder once the war is over. But how to arrive at democracy? To expect that the Kuomintang will practice self-denial and give up political power to its rivals or opponents is unthinkable, and the possibility of the rival groups being able to wrest that power from the Kuomintang is also remote. . . . Perhaps to practice democracy inside the Kuomintang is of more real significance than to try vainly to establish democracy for the country at large. If during the period of reconstruction the country shall continue in the hands of the Kuomintang, as it is not unlikely to do, it is evident that it will not be democratized before the Party itself is democratized."[7] He expresses the hope that the Kuomintang will find it in its interest to "prepare the country for a swift transition to democracy" and points out that the party has declared democracy to be its objective.

The People's Political Council[8]

The formation of the People's Political Council was symbolic of Chinese unity during the early period of the war. It first met on July 6, 1938 several months after the emergency congress of the Kuomintang passed a resolution calling for its creation. The new assembly had three main powers: to consider government policies and actions; to submit proposals to the government; and to question high government officials and receive reports from them. There were four categories of delegates or members, of which the two main groups—accounting for 188 out of the 200 members of the First People's Political Council—represented (1) provinces and municipalities, and (2) cultural and economic bodies and political activities. The Second and Third People's Political Councils have been essentially the same as the first in formal powers and organization, although there have been changes in the composition of the membership. The sessions are short—ten days in length—and the P.P.C. meets infrequently. The government may call an extra session or prolong a session, but has never used this power.

The First People's Political Council constituted a roster of outstanding personalities in Chinese political life. It contained not only many Kuomintang members but also seven representatives of the Communists, a number of figures from the National Salvation movement—including some persons who had been arrested for anti-Japanese activities before the war—and spokesmen for various lesser political groups. Although the proportions used in assigning delegates were far from exact,

[7] Chien, "War-Time Government in China," cited, pp. 869-71.

[8] Ibid., pp. 855-59. Linebarger, The China of Chiang K'ai-shek, cited, pp. 69-79. The Chinese Year Book, 1938-39, pp. 345-55. The Chinese Year Book, 1940-41, pp. 456-67. The China Year Book, 1939, pp. 230-37. "The People's Political Council," Contemporary China (New York, Chinese News Service), November 16, 1942.

every significant patriotic element in Chinese politics was represented, as well as some—Wang Ching-wei's adherents—that
later proved to be traitorous in character.

The nature of the sessions may be indicated by a brief sum-
mary of the second meeting of the First P.P.C., held in Chungking, October 28-November 6, 1938. In an introductory message,
Chiang Kai-shek urged continuance of the war with redoubled
effort. On October 30, Wang Ching-wei, who was then Chairman, proposed the formation of a General Proposals Examination Committee, consisting of all P.P.C. members, to consider
matters of extraordinary importance. This was undoubtedly
part of an effort by Wang to secure P.P.C. support for peace
moves. The motion was carried after careful consideration. On
November 1, the P.P.C. passed a resolution affirming faith in
Chiang Kai-shek—a significant move since the enemies of
resistance were then concentrating their fire on the Generalissimo. On November 2 the P.P.C. urged the creation of a new
war-time newspaper policy, in accordance with the Program of
Resistance and Reconstruction. It was suggested that censorship
be improved, through the affording of greater protection from
government interference and the adoption of measures to punish censors who exceeded their authority. On November 4 a
second resolution on this subject requested the discontinuance
of news censorship before publication. On November 5 the
General Proposals Examination Committee adopted many
resolutions of great military and political importance. Methods
of education were to be improved and special attention given
to military training in senior high schools and colleges. Speedy
development of rural industries was urged, in order to lay
an economic basis for prolonged resistance. Important changes
were recommended in the military service regulations, to elim-
inate abuses in certain provinces. The following day the P.P.C.
proposed that the government concentrate on the economic
rehabilitation of the Northwest and that forestry and horticul-
ture be improved both in the Northwest and Southwest. At the
end of the session a Resident Committee of 25, representing all
groups in the P.P.C., was elected to carry on until the next
meeting.

What is the significance of the work of the People's Political
Council for the development of democracy in China? Spokesmen for the government stress its importance as a halfway-house

between a public forum and a parliament. Others argue that the
P.P.C. is purely advisory in character, that there is no legal
definition of the nature of the measures that must be submitted
to it for approval, and that the government is consequently
free to act as it pleases. This leaves the P.P.C. with the power
to question officials as its only weapon—and a rather weak one.
Official spokesmen would probably reply that in the period
since the establishment of the P.P.C. a network of provincial
and district councils has been created, that these bodies now
elect many of the members of the national P.P.C. and that
the whole process is an example of slow development toward
democratic practices. On the other hand, it is a fact that the
use of this network makes for the inclusion of a larger number
of Kuomintang members than before.

The truth seems to be that the significance of the People's
Political Council—as an advisory body selected essentially by
the Kuomintang, whatever the forms of election may be—does
not lie in its formal organization or the powers officially given
to it, but in the general character of the Chinese political scene
at any particular moment. When the P.P.C. was created in 1938,
there was a greater freedom of speech than China had known
in many years, the unity of all groups was at a high level, and
the times were generally propitious for the new body to be a
sounding board of national opinion. That it served this function
at least to some degree is indicated by the importance of the
subjects that came before it for discussion and by the fact that
Wang Ching-wei considered it worth while to try to win the
Council over to his point of view.

At that time it was impossible to tell in what direction the
P.P.C. might develop—whether it would grow in stature and
become increasingly representative of all groups or whether it
would remain essentially an instrument by which "the Kuomintang provided a safety-valve for opposition without touching
the apparatus of its own power."[9] Today it is possible to look
back, with the political developments of the intervening half-
decade in mind, and to conclude that the P.P.C. has not grown
in significance, but has been overshadowed as a result of serious
changes in the trend of Chinese politics. There is no longer the
same freedom of speech in China and, while Chinese unity
continues, it does not have as inclusive a character as it possessed

[9] Linebarger, *The China of Chiang K'ai-shek*, cited, p. 72.

in the days when the defense of Hankow was being prepared. The P.P.C. has not been in a position to meet crucial economic, political and military issues effectively and has therefore declined in significance, although its position may improve if general conditions again become favorable.

Central Government and the Provinces*

The area of Free China is a more closely knit political and economic entity today than in 1937. The transfer of the National Government into the interior early in the war and the subsequent development of industry and agriculture in the Southwest have given the Central authorities an influence in the hinterland that was never possessed by the old Nanking regime. Unquestionably, this is far from being the whole picture, for Japanese invasion has created new problems by cutting Chungking off from more than two-fifths of its people in the invaded areas. Moreover, since guerrilla government behind the Japanese lines follows a pattern quite different from that of unoccupied China, there will be a serious question of integration after the war. Yet in the interior provinces as such there has been a process of unification in the past six and a half years.

This is true, for example, of the northwestern provinces of China proper, through which the Generalissimo made a month's trip in the summer of 1942. It is also true of Sinkiang, whose Governor, after many years of extremely close relations with the Soviet Union, has recently shown increasing signs of moving into the orbit of Central influence. But the most typical examples of the course of relations between Chungking and the provinces are to be found in Szechwan and Yunnan. The former is the seat of the national capital at Chungking and constitutes the main base of Chinese resistance. The latter has been of great significance as the province of the Burma Road and as China's southern defense against Japanese forces pressing in from Burma. In neither case has the path of subordination to Central authority been smooth, nor has the process gone nearly as far in Yunnan as in Szechwan.

The nature of pre-war relations between Nanking and Szechwan has already been suggested (see p. 12). When hostilities began in the summer of 1937, General Liu Hsiang, Szechwan leader who was working with the Central government,

* For the more recent state of Central-provincial relations, see p. 61.

pledged his support in resisting Japan. But his death at the beginning of 1938 precipitated a crisis in which the National authorities were able—although not without difficulty—to extend their influence within the province. It was necessary, however, to send a number of Central generals to Szechwan to explain matters to the local leaders. Two of the main difficulties appear to have been to adjust the conflicting ambitions of aspirants to office in the provincial government, and to persuade some of the local generals to send the forces under their command to the front. These were perhaps simply the forms in which the clash of national and provincial authority found expression.

While issues of this type were being raised, the war was introducing new economic and political influences. With the fall of Hankow at the end of October 1938, the entire governmental machinery was moved to Chungking. Plans were then drawn up for the establishment of new economic enterprises throughout the Southwest, especially in Szechwan. Chungking became the financial, political and economic center of Free China and more and more overshadowed Chengtu, the seat of the Szechwan government. In the summer of 1939 rumors began to spread about difficulties in Chengtu, one of the problems apparently being to decide who was to hold the post of Governor. The dilemma was met by Chiang Kai-shek's assuming the position. He was later succeeded by Chang Chun, a native of Szechwan and one of his right-hand men. This is an instance of the manner in which Central control over Szechwan has been greatly extended, despite the resistance of some provincial military, political and economic elements to Chungking's authority. War conditions and the growth of the national power have served to keep this opposition under control.

A similar picture is seen in Yunnan which before the war was perhaps the most autonomous province of China proper. Since 1937 Yunnan has undergone significant industrial changes—although industry is still at a very low level—and has made particular advances in the development of transportation. The provincial capital, Kunming, is second only to Chungking among Free China's economic centers. In dealing with the governor of Yunnan, General Lung Yun, the National Government, while extending its influence, has been careful to move slowly, so as not to step on provincial toes. This is particularly true because disaffection in this area could imperil the war of resistance. It is recalled that in December 1938, before leaving China, Wang Ching-wei sought to win Lung Yun over to the Japanese side. If Wang had succeeded, he would have had a Chinese base against the Central government, instead of being obliged to depend entirely on the enemy. His defection, instead of being a patent act of treachery, might then have been camouflaged as a mere difference of opinion with other elements in China.

The procedure followed by Chungking in dealing with Yunnan and other provinces is a combination of economic construction, military pressure and very skillful political maneuvering. The accent is first of all on closer relations with the central authority. Thus, in Yunnan corruption and backwardness are still very marked, but a degree of outside authority has been introduced. The provincial authorities, however, retain considerable power. At present, Yunnan, like the rest of China, is in the process of development, with everything depending on victory over Japan and the maintenance of Chinese unity in the postwar period.

Sinkiang, a vast Chinese province of less than four million people, lying in the far Northwest and bordering strategically on the U.S.S.R., Outer Mongolia, Tibet, India and Afghanistan, is another important example of the extension of Central authority into frontier territories. Until recently, Sinkiang's closest relations were with Russia, partly because communications were so much better with that country than with China or any other neighboring area; partly, because in 1934 the ruler of the province, General Sheng Shih-tsai, accepted Soviet military aid in maintaining his position against internal opponents. Consequently the Russians, although never denying China's sovereignty in Sinkiang, exerted great economic, political and military influence there in cooperation with the provincial government. The Chinese Central authorities, involved at first in civil war and later in war with Japan, had hardly any effective voice in provincial affairs. In 1942, however, following negotiations between Sheng Shih-tsai and envoys from Chungking, including Madame Chiang Kai-shek, the province made a shift in its external relations, drawing closer to the Chinese National Government. The Russians then withdrew, taking with them their garrison forces and all equipment used by them in the economic development of Sinkiang. The effect was to bring the province to a much greater degree under Chungking control although probably at considerable cost to Sinkiang's immediate economic development.

The Constitutional Movement

Constitutional rule is a symbol, in a historical sense, of the goal for which China is fighting. The early nationalist revolutionaries who opposed the Manchu regime regarded Western constitutionalism as one of their principal political aims—the touchstone of China's becoming a modern nation. Sun Yat-sen himself declared that the country must pass through three stages: military unification, political tutelage and constitutional government. Consequently, whatever the realities of Chinese politics may be at any particular moment, the history of the Kuomintang is closely linked with the objective of constitutional rule. Moreover, the Kuomintang has made many pledges to lead the country from the present phase of tutelage into the constitutional period.

In 1931 the government adopted a Provisional Constitution, under which, with some changes, it is still operating at the present time. Toward the end of the following year—at the proposal of Sun Fo, son of Sun Yat-sen—the Central Executive Committee of the Kuomintang decided that preparations should be made for the establishment of a permanent constitution. March 1935 was set as the date for the convocation of a National Congress, which was to adopt a constitution, but the meeting was later postponed. The Legislative Yuan, which was entrusted with the power to draft a document and to publish it for public comment, began its work early in 1933 and formally completed the draft in May 1936. The task had taken more than three years, and the document had gone through seven revisions. On May 5, 1936 the National Government formally promulgated the Draft Constitution.

When hostilities began in Shanghai in August 1937 over one-half of the almost 1700 delegates to the National Congress had been chosen. This body was scheduled to meet in November 1937, but was postponed indefinitely as a result of the outbreak of war. During the first year and a half of resistance—the period of active positional fighting for important centers—there was little discussion of early constitutional action. In fact, the extraordinary session of the Kuomintang in April 1938 declared in its manifesto: "Following the day when the war is won we should wind up military affairs and expedite the carrying out of constitutionalism. . . ."[10] But after the war entered the stalemate stage at the end of 1938, attention was again focussed on the constitutional question as an immediate issue.

When the People's Political Council met in September 1939, the Generalissimo, in cautious terms, expressed approval of the constitutional movement. The constitutional question was brought up in seven different proposals, introduced by councillors from the Kuomintang, Communist Party, National Socialist Party, Young China Party, Third Party, National Salvationists, and a group representing the Association for the Promotion of Vocational Education. These suggestions were combined in the following resolution passed by the Council:

> Petition the Government to announce the date for the convocation of the People's Congress, for the establishment of a constitution, for the formation of a constitutional government.
> Petition the Chairman to appoint a number of Council members as a constitutional committee to assist the present Government in its transformation to a constitutional democracy.
> Petition the Government to promulgate a law under which political equality is granted to all the peoples of the nation, except traitors.
> To meet the demands of the war situation, the Government organs are to be strengthened and improved in order to concentrate the talents of the nation on the work of resistance and reconstruction.[11]

The fact that the first two demands, relating to constitutional reform, were coupled with the last two, urging legal recognition of parties other than the Kuomintang and greater use of "the talents of the nation" in governmental operations, suggests that the latter were the main objectives sought by the Council in asking for constitutional action. In accordance with the resolution, the Generalissimo then appointed a "Constitutionalism Promotion Committee," containing representatives of all points of view within the People's Political Council. Following the session, many informal constitutional conferences were held in Chungking, Chengtu and other cities. In Chungking, for exam-

[10] *The People's Tribune*, April 1938, p. 69.
[11] "The People's Political Council: Its Past Work and Present Tasks," New China Information Committee, Bulletin No. 11 (January 1940), p. 38.

ple, twenty-five councillors sponsored an informal conference at which over one hundred editors, professors and educators were present.

The Draft Constitution consists of 147 articles in eight chapters. Chapter I defines the Republic of China, gives equality to all racial groups within it, and fixes the capital at Nanking. In Chapter II the rights and duties of citizens are explained. Every citizen is guaranteed liberty of person and various freedoms (domicile, changing of residence, speech, religious belief, secrecy of correspondence, etc.) without restriction "except in accordance with law." Chapter III outlines the organization of the National Congress, which is to be elected for a term of six years by universal suffrage and secret ballot of citizens of twenty or over. The Congress is to be convened every three years for one month by the President. Among other functions, it is to elect the President and Vice-President, President of the Legislative and Censor Yuan and the members of the Legislative and Censor Yuan. Chapter IV defines the organization of the Central Government, assigning great power to the President. Article 44 provides for circumstances under which he may issue orders of emergency. Chapter V deals with the organization of provinces, districts and municipalities, Chapter VI with the economic structure of a constitutional China, Chapter VII with education, and Chapter VIII with the enforcement and amendment of the Constitution.[12]

Since the Kuomintang Central Executive Committee decided in November 1939 to convene the National Congress a year later, the first nine months of 1940 saw widespread discussion of constitutional questions. Some circles opposed the move to adopt a constitution on the ground that action was not advisable under war conditions. Others urged the appropriateness of such a step as part of the process of winning the war. Still others, while agreeing with this view, argued for the modification of the constitutional draft in order to remove alleged imperfections and restrictions on democracy. But the heart of the matter was that the constitution provided a battleground for the continuing struggle among reactionary, conservative, liberal and radical points of view. The key question, as all understood, was not whether one or another provision was desirable, but whether, through the adoption of constitutional government, China

[12] For the text of the Draft Constitution, see Appendix, pp. 70-85.

would formally recognize the legality of groups outside the Kuomintang and strengthen the legal basis of individual liberties. It was true that, even with the constitution in operation, government might be undemocratic, but the existence of the constitution could itself be an instrument in the hands of those working for greater democracy.[13]

The attitude of Chinese liberals toward the status of the various political parties was expressed as follows by a Chinese editor:

It is felt by not a few thinking Chinese that the chief justification for the calling of the People's Congress this coming November to pass the Draft Constitution as the law of the land is to give an opportunity to every one and every party to contribute his and its best towards the winning of the present war. So long as a party is in the eyes of the law illegal, or is not given legal standing, so long is it impossible to expect the members of such a party to give of their best materially and spiritually. . . . If the forthcoming People's Congress will initiate constitutional government in China, by giving *de jure* recognition to all parties which are now cooperating with the National Government, then for this reason alone, if for no other, it will have more than justified its creation.[14]

The opposite point of view was expressed in these words:

"The people of the country must know that present-day China is a San Min Chu I revolutionary unit, unlike the English and American States in which 'parties divide the spoils.' According to the Tsung-li's[15] principle of national reconstruction, all groups outside our party are illegal associations. . . . According to the teachings bequeathed by the Tsung-li, the realization of constitutional government not only does not mean the winding up of party rule, not only cannot initiate the liberation of proscribed parties, but marks a step forward in the expansion of rule by our party's principles over the whole country. The realization of constitutional government in one province will come after all the hsien [district] divisions in that province have completed local self-government in accordance with the principles of our party; the realization of constitutional government in the entire country will come after all places in the

[13] For criticisms of particular features of the Draft Constitution from a liberal viewpoint, see Appendix, pp. 104-110. See also: Sa Chien-li, "Views on the Draft Constitution" (Tui Yü Hsien Fa Ts'ao An I Chien), in *Ch'üan Min K'ang Chan Chou K'an*, November 4, 1939, pp. 1400-1401. Opposing arguments are presented in *Hsien Cheng Chih Yueh K'an*, January 1, 1940, "Special Number on Constitutional Government."

[14] Wen Yuan-ning, "Editorial Commentary," *T'ien Hsia Monthly* (Shanghai), May 1940, p. 408.

[15] Tsung-li is a title often used in referring to Sun Yat-sen.

country have completed local self-government in accordance with the principles of our party."[16]

By the end of June 1940 more than three-quarters of the delegates to the National Congress had been chosen, but in September the meeting was cancelled. The reasons given by the government for the postponement were expressed as follows in a semi-official publication:

". . . it soon became clear that, on account of communication and other difficulties, it would be well nigh impossible for the delegates to reach Chungking in time, especially as many of them had to come from the occupied area. . . . The closure of the Burma Road in July was a contributing factor in that it made it necessary for the government to devote its primary attention to the prosecution of war in a much more difficult international situation."[17]

Thereafter the matter was dropped, but at the plenary session of the Kuomintang Central Executive Committee in September 1943, Chiang Kai-shek suggested the importance of preparing for constitutional government after the war. With the establishment of representative institutions, he said, the Kuomintang would lose all special privileges, and other parties would be equal to it in rights and freedoms. The session passed a resolution providing that within one year after the conclusion of the war the National Government was to convene a National Congress to adopt and promulgate a constitution. The National Congress was also to designate a date when the constitution would come into effect. A Committee for the Establishment of Constitutional Government was named by the Generalissimo in October. Of its 53 members 49 belonged to the Kuomintang, 2 to the Communist Party, and one each to the National Socialist and Chinese Youth Parties. The Committee's function was to consider all matters concerning the preparation and enforcement of constitutionalism and to submit proposals to the Government.

In the United States these moves toward constitutional government were welcomed as signs of Chungking's democratic

[16] Liu Chen-tung, "Constitutional Government and Party Rule" (Hsien Cheng Yü Tang Chih), *Hsin Cheng Chih Yueh K'an*, January 1, 1940, p. 4. The reference in this quotation to hsien, or district, government relates to Chungking's program for developing local administration. See *The Chinese Year Book, 1940-41*, pp. 490-92, and Chiang Kai-shek, *Resistance and Reconstruction* (New York, Harper, 1943), pp. 183-97.

[17] *China After Four Years of War* (Hong Kong, The China Publishing Co., 1941) p. 39.

intentions in the post-war period. Indeed, there was a sense of relief in editorial comment on the subject, for the Central Executive Committee's announcement came at a time of disquieting rumors about Japanese peace moves and possible recurrence of civil war in China. There was in the United States no disposition to underestimate China's role in the war with Japan; in fact, the desire was widespread to accord China the fullest equality as a member of the Big Four of the United Nations. But concern did exist about some of the tendencies manifesting themselves in Chungking. Any action that pointed in the direction of a democratic, progressive China, playing its proper part in international affairs, was therefore certain to be welcomed by the American public.

POSTSCRIPT

In the period since the preceding chapters were written Japan's continuing military successes on the China front have produced a major political crisis in Chungking. The Generalissimo's prestige has suffered, even though he remains the most important man in China; and tendencies toward provincial autonomy have again become marked. In September 1944 the People's Political Council convened in an atmosphere of relaxed censorship and criticized the government sharply. Within a few weeks, however, strict controls of speech and press were again being enforced. Late in October General Joseph W. Stilwell's recall from China at the Generalissimo's request caused widespread American discussion of Chungking's shortcomings. On November 20, as part of a significant cabinet shakeup, the most widely criticized members of the régime— War Minister Ho Ying-chin, Education Minister Chen Li-fu and Finance Minister H. H. Kung—gave up these posts. Most important was Ho's replacement by the progressive general, Chen Cheng. Although the changes were not decisive—partly because the three men continued to hold other high positions —the reorganization did suggest that Chungking might move toward the adoption of new policies. The crucial unanswered question was whether a coalition government of national unity, including the Kuomintang, Communists and members of lesser political groups, would be formed in one of the gravest hours of the war.

December 2, 1944

DOCUMENTS

THE WILL OF DR. SUN YAT-SEN[1]

This last testament of the father of the Chinese Republic is read every Monday at weekly memorial meetings in Kuomintang branches, government offices, party committee meetings, schools, barracks and factories.

I have served the cause of the People's Revolution for forty years, during which time my object has consistently been to secure liberty and equality for our country. From the experience of these forty years, I have come to realize that, in order to reach this object, it is necessary to awaken the masses of our people, and to join hands with those countries which are prepared to treat us as equals in our fight for the common cause of humanity.

At present, we have not yet completed the work of the Revolution, and it is my sincere hope that our comrades will continue to fight for the ultimate realization of our goal, in accordance with the Principles of National Reconstruction, the Program of National Reconstruction, the San Min Doctrine, and the Declaration of the First National Convention, all of which have been drawn up by myself. Recently I have proposed the convening of a national people's conference and the abolition of unequal treaties; you should especially work toward the realization of these aims within the shortest possible period of time.

The above is my will

Sun Wen

Signed on March 11
    Taken down by Wang Ching-wei, February 24
    Fourteenth Year of the Republic of China

Witnesses:

T. V. Soong	Wu Ching-heng
Sun Fo	Ho Hsiang-ying
Shao Yuan-ch'ung	Tai Chi-tao
Tai En-shai	Tsui Lu

[1] Reproduced in *Sun Yat-sen*, by Leonard S. Hsu, University of Southern California Press, 1933.

COMMUNIST DECLARATION ON UNITY (1935)[1]

Issued on August 31, 1935 by the Chinese Soviet Government and the Central Committee of the Chinese Communist Party.

To men and women in all walks of life—labor, industry, agriculture, military affairs, politics, commerce and education—in China as well as abroad:

Japanese imperialism is increasing its offensive against our country. Step by step the treacherous Nanking government is continuing its capitulation to Japan. Following the fate of the four north-eastern provinces [the three provinces in Manchuria and that of Jehol—*Editor*], our northern provinces [Chahar, Hopei, Shansi, Suiyuan and Shantung—*Editor*] are virtually lost.

Peiping and Tientsin, cities which have been centers of culture for thousands of years; Hopei, Shansi, Honan, Shantung and other provinces which have unlimited natural resources; Chahar, Suiyuan and other territories which have most decisive strategic significance; the Peiping-Mukden, Peiping-Hankow, Peiping-Pukow, Peiping-Suiyuan and other railroads which hold the threads of the political and economic life of all China—all of these are virtually under the control of the Japanese military forces. The headquarters of the Japanese Kwantung Army is actively carrying out the plan of creating "Mongolkuo" and "Hwapeikuo" [Japanese puppet states in Mongolia and north China—*Editor*]. Since the Japanese invasion of Manchuria in 1931 Japan has advanced from Manchuria to Jehol, from Jehol to the Great Wall, from the Great Wall to the "Luantung Demilitarized Region" and from that region to the virtual occupation of Hopei, Chahar, Suiyuan and other northern provinces.

During this period of less than four years, a large part of the territory of China has been occupied by the Japanese invaders. The vicious plan for the complete annexation of our country, sketched out in the Tanaka memorandum, is being systematically carried through. If this aggression continues, our provinces in the Yangtze and Pearl valleys [central and south China—*Editor*] and other remaining territories will also gradually be seized by the Japanese plunderers. And with this, our country, which possesses a history of five thousand years, will be completely transformed into a colony and our 450,000,000 countrymen will be wholly enslaved.

[1] *China Today* (New York) December 1935, pp. 58-59.

In the last few years our country and our nation has been placed in a most precarious situation. Resistance to the Japanese invasion means the road to life, while non-resistance means the road to death. To resist the Japanese invasion and save our country has become the "holy duty" of every Chinese citizen.

But the most regrettable fact is that among our great people there exists a handful of corrupt elements who have "human faces, but beastly hearts"—Chiang Kai-shek, Wang Ching-wei, Chang Hsueh-liang, and other traitors; Yang Yung-tai, Huang Fu, Wang I-tang, Chang Chung and other old agents of Japanese imperialism. All of them have betrayed our country by their policy of "non-resistance," they have advocated acceptance of the Japanese demands under the slogan of "meet reverses by submission." They carry on civil war and suppress all anti-imperialist movements with demagogic propaganda—"In order to resist external enemies, internal order must be achieved first." They have prevented the people from resisting Japan by deceitful slogans—"Ten years of propagation," "Ten years of education," "Prepare for revenge." They have forced our people to wait for destruction with the treacherous tactics of "Wait for the outbreak of the second World War."

Recently these traitors to their native land, under the slogans of "Sino-Japanese friendship and cooperation" and "Pan-Asianism" have carried out an openly corrupt and disgraceful policy of capitulation, unmatched either in the history of China or of the world. The Japanese imperialists demanded the withdrawal of the troops of Yu Hsueh-chung, Sung Chih-yuan and others from north China, and all of these troops were immediately withdrawn to the south and the west to carry on an internecine war against their own people. The Japanese imperialists demanded the removal of certain political and military officials, and all of these officials were immediately removed from their posts. The Japanese imperialists demanded the removal of the Hopei provincial government from Tientsin, and it was immediately transferred to Paoting. The Japanese plunderers demanded the banning of Chinese newspapers and journals which did not suit them, and all these papers and journals were immediately banned. The Japanese imperialists demanded the punishment of the editor of the *New Life Weekly*, and other editors and correspondents of Chinese newspapers and journals, and immediately all these people were subjected to arrest and imprisonment. The Japanese imperialists demanded the introduction into Chinese schools and universities of the slave system of pro-Japanese education, and all advanced Chinese literature was immediately burned; numerous honest boys and girls, who did not want to become the slaves of an alien state, were either arrested or executed. The Japanese imperialists demanded that the Japanese should be invited as counsellors in all Chinese state institutions, and Chiang Kai-shek immediately opened the doors of all these institutions to Japanese spies. The Japanese imperialists even demanded the disbanding of the Kuomintang organization, and its local organizations in north China and in Amoy were immediately disbanded. The Japanese imperialists demanded the disbanding of the "Blue Shirt" organization, and its leaders in north China, Tsen Kwang-ching and Chiang Hsiao-hsien, immediately resigned their posts.

The Chinese Soviet Government and the Communist Party of China recognize that the acts of the Japanese plunderers and Chinese traitors are an unparalleled disgrace to the Chinese nation. The Soviet Government and the Communist Party emphatically declare, "We not only vigorously oppose the invasion of our territory and interference in our internal political affairs by the Japanese imperialists, but we also strongly protest against the Japanese demands for the disbanding of the Kuomintang and 'Blue Shirt' organizations." From the viewpoint of the Communist Party and the Soviet Government, all the affairs of the Chinese people should be handled by the Chinese themselves. No matter how great the crimes committed by the Kuomintang and the "Blue Shirt" organizations, the Japanese should certainly have no voice in the matter.

Province after province is being occupied by foreign invaders. Millions upon millions of citizens are being enslaved. City after city, village after village is being washed with blood. Emigrants abroad are everywhere being persecuted and deported. Internal as well as foreign affairs are being dictated by our enemies. How can this be called a state! How can this be called a nation!

Fellow countrymen! Ethiopia, with a meager population of eight million, is offering armed resistance to Italian imperialism in defence of her territory and people; then can a great country like ours, with a population of four hundred million, fold its hands and wait for death? The Soviet Government and the Communist Party firmly believe that with the exception of a handful of traitors and agents of the Japanese imperialists, who are willing to follow the example of Li Wang-yun, Cheng Hsiao-shu, Chang Ching-hwei and Henry Pu Yi, the absolute majority of our countrymen in all walks of life—labor, industry, agriculture, military affairs, commerce and education—refuse to become the slaves of the Japanese imperialists. The declaration of war of the Chinese Soviet Government against Japan; the repeated proposals of the Chinese Red Army to all armies throughout the country for a united resistance to the Japanese invasion; the bitter struggles of the Northern Expeditionary Anti-Japanese Vanguard of the Red Army under the most difficult circumstances; the bloody battles of the 19th Route Army and the masses of Shanghai against the Japanese forces in 1932; the heroic armed struggles of the soldiers and people of Chahar, the Great Wall region and other places against the Japanese invaders; the acceptance of the proposals of the Chinese Red Army for a united front against Japan by the Fukien People's Government; the noble sacrifices of the national heroes who gave up their lives for the sake of the salvation of China—Lo Tung-hsien, Hsu Ming-hung, Chi Hung-chang, Teng Tieh-mei, Pei Yang, Tung Chang-yung, Pan Hung-sen, Sze Tsan-tang, Chu Chiu-pei, Sun Yun-ching, Fang Chih-min, etc., and of those who were imprisoned for the same cause—Liu Chung-wu, Tien Han, Tu Chung-yuan and other patriots; the strenuous struggles of the anti-Japanese boycott; strikes, demonstrations and other movements carried on by workers, peasants, merchants, students and others for the salvation of China for the past few years, especially the continuous struggles of tens of thousands of armed anti-Japanese fighters in the northeast, led by Yang Shing-yu, Chao Shang-tze, Wang Te-kung, Li Yen-lo, Chou Pao-chung, Hsia Wen-yung, Wu Yi-cheng, Li Hwa-tang and other national heroes—all these show that victory for the movement against the Japanese invasion and the salvation of our country can be achieved. So far our countrymen have not yet achieved the victories which they deserve; this is due on the one hand to the joint attacks of the Japanese imperialists from outside and Chiang Kai-shek from within, and on the other, to the absence of unity among all anti-Japanese and anti-Chiang Kai-shek forces because of lack of contact and various misunderstandings.

Therefore, at this time, when the destruction of our nation is so imminent, the Communist Party and Soviet Government once more appeal to all our countrymen—regardless of the differences of political opinion and interests that have existed or may still exist between political parties and groups, regardless of the differences of opinion and interests between various groups, regardless of the conflicts that have taken place or are taking place between different armies—to be awake to the necessity of "stopping the quarrels among brothers inside the wall to meet invaders from outside" [an old Chinese proverb.—Editor]. First of all we must stop the internecine war in order to unify the strength of the whole nation (man power, material and financial resources, armed forces, etc.) to fight for the defeat of the Japanese invaders and the liberation of China. The Soviet Government and the Communist Party once again declare—: "If the Kuomintang armies will stop their attacks on the Soviet districts and if their forces will fight the Japanese invasion, then, regardless of the animosity and differences of opinion on internal problems that have existed between them and the Red Army in the past, the Red Army will not only immediately cease its action against them, but is ready to join hands with them to carry on a joint fight for the salvation of our country. The Soviet Government and Communist Party now make the following appeal:

"All countrymen who are not willing to be enslaved!

All sincere military officers and soldiers!

All members of political parties and organizations, and all who are willing to participate in the movement against the Japanese invasion and for the salvation of China!

All the Kuomintang youth and "Blue Shirt" organizations who are nationally-minded!

All Chinese emigrants who are concerned about their fatherland!

All oppressed nationalities in China! (Mongolians, Mohammedans, Koreans, Miaos, Tibetans, Lolos, Yaos, Fans, etc.)

All arise! Smash through the thousand-fold oppressions of the Japanese imperialists and Chiang Kai-shek, and valiantly fight together with the Chinese Soviet Government and anti-Japanese governments in various places in the northeast for the formation of a united national defense government! Form a united anti-Japanese army with the Red Army and the Northeastern Peoples Army and all anti-Japanese volunteers!"

The Soviet Government and the Communist Party are willing to initiate this national defense government and are willing to discuss and negotiate with all organizations (trade unions, peasant unions, student associations, chambers of commerce, educational associations, newspaper unions, teachers unions, fraternal organizations, Chinese Masons, National Armed Defense Associations, Anti-Japanese Alliances, Associations for the Salvation of China, etc.), all prominent people, scholars and politicians, and all local military and administrative units—in a word, with all those who are willing to participate in the mission of fighting against the Japanese invasion and for the salvation of China. The national defense government formed as a result of such negotiations should be the provisional leading organ of the struggle for national existence. It should devise ways and means of calling together the real representatives of all our countrymen (representatives of people of all walks of life democratically elected by labor, industry, the army, politics, commerce and education, and all parties, groups and organizations which are against Japan and for the salvation of China) to discuss more concretely all problems in connection with the fight to save China from Japanese aggression. The Soviet Government and the Communist Party will unconditionally and energetically support the convocation of such a people's representative organ, because the Soviet Government and the Communist Party will unconditionally carry out the resolutions of such an organ, because the Soviet Government and the Communist Party unconditionally respect the public opinion of the people.

The main task of the national defense government should be resistance to Japan and the salvation of our country. Its political program should include the following points:—

1. Resistance to Japanese invasion and the recovery of lost territories.

2. Assistance to the famine-stricken; the undertaking of extensive river conservancy work for the purpose of preventing inundations and drought.

3. Confiscation of all the properties of the Japanese imperialists in China to finance the war against the Japanese invasion.

4. Confiscation of all the properties, stored food and land owned by the traitors and the agents of the Japanese imperialists, to be used by the poor countrymen and anti-Japanese fighters.

5. Abolition of onerous taxes and fees, reorganization of finance and currency, and the development of industry, agriculture and commerce.

6. Increase of the salaries, wages, and soldiers' pay and improvement of living conditions of workers, peasants, soldiers, students, teachers, etc.

7. Exercise of democratic rights and liberation of all political prisoners.

8. Free education and provision of jobs for the unemployed youth.

9. Equality for all nationalities residing in the territories of China. Protection of the life, property, and freedom of residence and business of the Chinese emigrants abroad.

10. Union with all anti-imperialist elements—the toiling people of Japan, Korea, Formosa and other oppressed nations—as our allies. Union with all nations which are sympathetic to the liberation movement of the Chinese nation, and the establishment of friendly relations with those nations which maintain good-will and a neutral attitude toward this movement.

The united anti-Japanese army should be composed of all armed forces willing to resist Japan, and a central commanding staff of that army should be organized under the leadership of the national defense government. This staff should be composed of delegates elected by the anti-Japanese commanders and soldiers of all armies, or it should be organized through such other forms as may be decided by delegates representing all shades of public opinion. The Red Army will be the first to join unconditionally the united army to fight against the Japanese invasion and for the liberation of our country.

In order to enable the national defense government to bear the heavy responsibility of national defense, and the united army to fight against the Japanese invasion, the Communist Party and Soviet

Government call upon all fellow-countrymen who have money to contribute money, who have weapons to contribute weapons, who have food stores to contribute food, who are able to work to contribute work, who are experts and professionals to contribute services. The Communist Party and the Soviet Government firmly believe that if we, four hundred million countrymen, have a united national defense government to lead us, a united army to act as our vanguard, millions of armed masses as reserves, and countless numbers of the proletarians and masses in the Far East and all over the world as our allies, then we can certainly defeat Japanese aggression which is opposed by its own people in Japan and by the powers abroad!

Fellow countrymen! Arise!

Fight for the life of our Fatherland!

Fight for the existence of our nation!

Fight for the independence of our country!

Fight for our territorial integrity!

Fight for our human rights and liberties!

Long live the unity of the Chinese nation for the struggle against Japanese imperialism and for national existence!

The Chinese Soviet Government
Central Committee, Communist Party of China

August 31, 1935.

PROPOSED DRAFT CONSTITUTION (1936-37)[1]

The original draft constitution drawn up by the Legislative Yuan was made public on May 5, 1936. The following text, issued on April 30, 1937, differs from the 1936 version in the omission of one article which granted the People's Congress that adopted the Constitution the power to act as the first People's Congress under the Constitution.

By virtue of the mandate received from the whole body of citizens and in accordance with the bequeathed teachings of Dr. Sun, Founder of the Republic of China, the People's Congress of the Republic of China hereby ordains and enacts this Constitution and causes it to be promulgated throughout the land for faithful and perpetual observance by all.

CHAPTER I. GENERAL PROVISIONS

Article 1. The Republic of China is a *SAN MIN CHU I* Republic.

Article 2. The sovereignty of the Republic of China is vested in the whole body of its citizens.

Article 3. Persons having acquired the nationality of the Republic of China are citizens of the Republic of China.

Article 4. The territory of the Republic of China consists of areas originally constituting Kiangsu, Chekiang, Anhwei, Kiangsi, Hupeh, Hunan, Szechwan, Sikang, Hopei, Shantung, Shansi, Honan, Shensi, Kansu, Chinghai, Fukien, Kwangtung, Kwangsi, Yunnan, Kweichow, Liaoning, Kirin, Heilungkiang, Jehol, Chahar, Suiyuan, Ningsia, Sinkiang, Mongolia and Tibet.

The territory of the Republic of China shall not be altered except by resolution of the People's Congress.

Article 5. All races of the Republic of China are component parts of the Chinese Nation and shall be equal.

Article 6. The National Flag of the Republic of China shall have a red background with a blue sky and white sun in the upper left corner.

Article 7. The National Capital of the Republic of China shall be at Nanking.

[1] *T'ien Hsia Monthly* (Hongkong), May 1940, pp. 493-506.

CHAPTER II. RIGHTS AND DUTIES OF THE CITIZENS

Article 8. All citizens of the Republic of China shall be equal before the law.

Article 9. Every citizen shall enjoy the liberty of the person. Except in accordance with law, no one may be arrested, detained, tried or punished.

When a citizen is arrested or detained on suspicion of having committed a criminal act, the authority responsible for such action shall immediately inform the citizen himself and his relatives of the cause for his arrest or detention and shall, within a period of twenty-four hours, send him to a competent court of trial. The citizen so arrested or detained, or any one else, may also petition the court to demand from the authority responsible for such action the surrender, within twenty-four hours, of his person to the court for trial.

The court shall not reject such a petition; nor shall the responsible authority refuse to execute such a writ as mentioned in the preceding paragraph.

Article 10. With the exception of those in active military service, no one may be subject to military jurisdiction.

Article 11. Every citizen shall have the freedom of domicile; no private abode may be forcibly entered, searched or sealed except in accordance with law.

Article 12. Every citizen shall have the freedom to change his residence; such freedom shall not be restricted except in accordance with law.

Article 13. Every citizen shall have the freedom of speech, writing and publication; such freedom shall not be restricted except in accordance with law.

Article 14. Every citizen shall have the freedom of secrecy of correspondence; such freedom shall not be restricted except in accordance with law.

Article 15. Every citizen shall have the freedom of religious belief; such freedom shall not be restricted except in accordance with law.

Article 16. Every citizen shall have the freedom of assembly and of forming associations; such freedom shall not be restricted except in accordance with law.

Article 17. No private property shall be requisitioned, expropriated, sealed or confiscated except in accordance with law.

Article 18. Every citizen shall have the right to present petitions, lodge complaints and institute legal proceedings in accordance with law.

Article 19. Every citizen shall have the right to exercise, in accordance with law, the powers of election, recall, initiative and referendum.

Article 20. Every citizen shall have the right to compete, in accordance with law, in state examinations.

Article 21. Every citizen shall, in accordance with law, be amenable to the duty of paying taxes.

Article 22. Every citizen shall, in accordance with law, be amenable to the duty of performing military service.

Article 23. Every citizen shall, in accordance with law, be amenable to the duty of rendering public service.

Article 24. All other liberties and rights of the citizens which are not detrimental to public peace and order or public welfare shall be guaranteed by the Constitution.

Article 25. Only laws imperative for safeguarding national security, averting a national crisis, maintaining public peace and order or promoting public interest may restrict the citizens' liberties and rights.

Article 26. Any public functionary who illegally infringes upon any private liberty or right, shall, besides being subject to disciplinary punishment, be responsible under criminal and civil law. The injured person may also, in accordance with law, claim indemnity from the State for damages sustained.

Chapter III. The People's Congress

Article 27. The People's Congress shall be constituted of delegates elected as follows:

1. Each district, municipality or area of an equivalent status shall elect one delegate, but in case its population exceeds 300,000, one additional delegate shall be elected for every additional 500,000 people. The status of areas to be equivalent to a district or municipality shall be defined by law.

2. The number of delegates to be elected from Mongolia and Tibet shall be determined by law.

3. The number of delegates to be elected by Chinese citizens residing abroad shall be determined by law.

Article 28. Delegates to the People's Congress shall be elected by universal, equal, and direct suffrage and by secret ballots.

Article 29. Citizens of the Republic of China having attained the age of twenty years shall, in accordance with law, have the right to elect delegates. Citizens having attained the age of twenty-five years shall, in accordance with law, have the right to be elected delegates.

Article 30. The term of office of Delegates of the People's Congress shall be six years.

When a Delegate is found guilty of violation of a law or neglect of his duty, his constituency shall recall him in accordance with law.

Article 31. The People's Congress shall be convened by the President once every three years. Its session shall last one month, but may be extended another month when necessary.

Extraordinary sessions of the People's Congress may be convened at the instance of two-fifths or more of its members.

The President may convene extraordinary sessions of the People's Congress.

The People's Congress shall meet at the place where the Central Government is.

Article 32. The powers and functions of the People's Congress shall be as follows:

1. To elect the President and Vice-President of the Republic, the President of the Legislative Yuan, the President of the Censor Yuan, the Members of the Legislative Yuan and the Members of the Censor Yuan.

2. To recall the President and Vice-President of the Republic, the President of the Legislative Yuan, the President of the Judicial Yuan, the President of the Examination Yuan, the President of the Censor Yuan, the Members of the Legislative Yuan and the Members of the Censor Yuan.

3. To initiate laws.

4. To hold referenda on laws.

5. To amend the Constitution.

6. To exercise such other powers as are conferred by the Constitution.

Article 33. Delegates to the People's Congress shall not be held responsible outside of Congress for opinions they may express and votes they may cast during the session of Congress.

Article 34. Without the permission of the People's Congress, no delegate shall be arrested or detained during the session except when apprehended in *flagrante delicto*.

Article 35. The organization of the People's Congress and the election as well as recall of its Delegates shall be determined by law.

CHAPTER IV. THE CENTRAL GOVERNMENT

Section 1. The President

Article 36. The President is the Head of the State and represents the Republic of China in foreign relations.

Article 37. The President commands the land, sea and air forces of the whole country.

Article 38. The President shall, in accordance with law, promulgate laws and issue orders with the counter-signature of the President of the Yuan concerned.

Article 39. The President shall, in accordance with law, exercise the power of declaring war, negotiating peace and concluding treaties.

Article 40. The President shall, in accordance with law, declare and terminate a state of emergency.

Article 41. The President shall, in accordance with law, exercise the power of granting amnesties, special pardons, remission of sentences and restoration of civil rights.

Article 42. The President shall, in accordance with law, appoint and remove civil and military officials.

Article 43. The President shall, in accordance with law, confer honors and award decorations.

Article 44. In case the State is confronted with an emergency, or the economic life of the State meets with a grave danger, which calls for immediate action, the President, following the resolution of the Executive Meeting, may issue orders of emergency and do whatever is necessary to cope with the situation, provided that he shall submit his action to the ratification of the Legislative Yuan within three months after the issuance of the orders.

Article 45. The President may call meetings of the Presidents of the five Yuan to confer on matters relating to two or more Yuan, or on such matters as the President may bring out for consultation.

Article 46. The President shall be responsible to the People's Congress.

Article 47. Citizens of the Republic of China, having attained the age of forty years, may be elected President or Vice-President of the Republic.

Article 48. The election of the President and Vice-President shall be provided for by law.

Article 49. The President and Vice-President shall hold office for a term of six years and may be re-elected for a second term.

Article 50. The President shall, on the day of his inauguration, take the following oath:

"I do solemnly and sincerely swear before the people that I will observe the Constitution, faithfully perform my duties, promote the welfare of the people, safeguard the security of the State and be loyal to the trust of the people. Should I break my oath, I will submit myself to the most severe punishment the law may provide."

Article 51. When the Presidency is vacant, the Vice-President shall succeed to the office.

When the President is for some reason unable to attend to his duties, the Vice-President shall act for him. If both the President and the Vice-President are incapacitated, the President of the Executive Yuan shall discharge the duties of the President's office.

Article 52. The President shall retire from office on the day his term expires. If by that time a new President has not been inducted into office, the President of the Executive Yuan shall discharge the duties of the President's office.

Article 53. The period for the President of the Executive Yuan to discharge the duties of the President's office shall not exceed six months.

Article 54. Except in case of an offense against the internal or external security of the State, the President shall not be liable to criminal prosecution until he has been recalled or has retired from office.

Section 2. The Executive Yuan

Article 55. The Executive Yuan is the highest organ through which the Central Government exercises its executive powers.

Article 56. In the Executive Yuan, there shall be a President, a Vice-President and a number of Executive Members, to be appointed and removed by the President.

The Executive Members mentioned in the preceding paragraph who do not take charge of Ministries or Commissions shall not exceed half of those who are in charge of Ministries or Commissions as provided in the first paragraph of Article 58.

Article 57. In the Executive Yuan, there shall be various Ministries and Commissions which shall separately exercise their respective executive powers.

Article 58. The Ministers of the various Ministries and the Chairmen of the various Commissions shall be appointed by the President from among the Executive Members.

The President and the Vice-President of the Executive Yuan may act concurrently as Minister or Chairman mentioned in the preceding paragraph.

Article 59. The President of the Executive Yuan, the Executive Members, the Ministers of the various Ministries and the Chairmen of the various Commissions shall be individually responsible to the President.

Article 60. In the Executive Yuan there shall be Executive Meetings composed of the President, the President of the Executive Yuan and the Executive Members to be presided over by the President. In case the President is unable to be present, the President of the Executive Yuan shall preside.

Article 61. The following matters shall be decided at an Executive Meeting:

1. Statutory and budgetary bills to be submitted to the Legislative Yuan.

2. Bills concerning a state of emergency and special pardons to be submitted to the Legislative Yuan.

3. Bills concerning declaration of war, negotiation of peace, conclusion of treaties and other important international affairs to be submitted to the Legislative Yuan.

4. Matters of common concern to the various Ministries and Commissions.

5. Matters submitted by the President.

6. Matters submitted by the President of the Executive Yuan, the Executive Members, the various Ministries and Commissions.

Article 62. The organization of the Executive Yuan shall be determined by law.

Section 3. The Legislative Yuan

Article 63. The Legislative Yuan is the highest organ through which the Central Government exercises its legislative powers. It shall be responsible to the People's Congress.

Article 64. The Legislative Yuan shall have the power to decide on measures concerning legislation, budgets, a state of emergency, special pardons, declaration of war, negotiation of peace, conclusion of treaties and other important international affairs.

Article 65. In the discharge of its duties the Legislative Yuan may interrogate the various Yuan, Ministries and Commissions.

Article 66. In the Legislative Yuan, there shall be a President who shall hold office for a term of three years and may be eligible for re-election.

Article 67. In regard to the election of Members of the Legislative Yuan, the Delegates of the various provinces, Mongolia, Tibet and of citizens residing abroad, to the People's Congress shall separately hold a preliminary election to nominate their respective candidates and submit a list of their names to the Congress for election. The candidates are not confined to the Delegates to the People's Congress. The respective number of candidates shall be proportioned as follows:

1. A province with a population of less than 5,000,000 shall nominate four candidates. A province with a population of more than 5,000,000 but less than 10,000,000 shall nominate six candidates. A province with a population of more than 10,000,000, but less than 15,000,000 shall nominate eight candidates. A province with a population of more than 15,000,000 but less than 20,000,000 shall nominate ten candidates. A province with a population of more than 20,000,000 but less than 25,000,000 shall nominate twelve

candidates. A province with a population of more than 25,000,000 but less than 30,000,000 shall nominate fourteen candidates. A province with a population of more than 30,000,000 shall nominate sixteen candidates.

2. Mongolia and Tibet shall each nominate eight candidates.

3. Citizens residing abroad shall nominate eight candidates.

Article 68. Members of the Legislative Yuan shall hold office for a term of three years and may be eligible for re-election.

Article 69. The Executive Yuan, Judicial Yuan, Examination Yuan, and Censor Yuan may submit to the Legislative Yuan measures concerning matters within their respective jurisdiction.

Article 70. The President may, before the promulgation or execution of a legislative measure, request the Legislative Yuan to reconsider it.

If the Legislative Yuan, with regard to the request for consideration, should decide to maintain the original measure by a two-thirds vote of the Members present, the President shall promulgate or execute it without delay; provided that in case of a bill of law or a treaty, the President may submit it to the People's Congress for a referendum.

Article 71. The President shall promulgate a measure presented by the Legislative Yuan for promulgation within thirty days after its receipt.

Article 72. Members of the Legislative Yuan shall not be held responsible outside of the said Yuan for opinions they may express and votes they may cast during its session.

Article 73. Without the permission of the Legislative Yuan, no member may be arrested or detained except when apprehended in *flagrante delicto*.

Article 74. No Member of the Legislative Yuan may concurrently hold any other public office or engage in any business or profession.

Article 75. The election of Members of the Legislative Yuan and the organization of the Legislative Yuan shall be determined by law.

Section 4.   The Judicial Yuan

Article 76. The Judicial Yuan is the highest organ through which the Central Government exercises its judicial powers. It shall attend to the adjudication of civil, criminal and administrative suits, the discipline and punishment of public functionaries and judicial administration.

Article 77. In the Judicial Yuan, there shall be a President who shall hold office for a term of three years. He shall be appointed by the President,

The President of the Judicial Yuan shall be responsible to the People's Congress.

Article 78. Matters concerning special pardons, remission of sentence and restoration of civil rights shall be submitted to the President for action by the President of the Judicial Yuan in accordance with law.

Article 79. The Judicial Yuan shall have the power to unify the interpretation of statutes and ordinances.

Article 80. Judicial officials shall, in accordance with law, have perfect independence in the conduct of trials.

Article 81. No judicial official may be removed from office unless he has been subject to criminal or disciplinary punishment or declared an interdicted person; nor may a judicial official be suspended or transferred, or have his salary reduced except in accordance with law.

Article 82. The organization of the Judicial Yuan and the various Courts of Justice shall be determined by law.

Section 5.   The Examination Yuan

Article 83. The Examination Yuan is the highest organ through which the Central Government exercises its examination powers. It shall attend to the selection of civil service candidates by examination and to the registration of persons qualified for public service.

Article 84. In the Examination Yuan there shall be a President who shall hold office for a term of three years, to be appointed by the President.

The President of the Examination Yuan shall be responsible to the People's Congress.

Article 85. The Examination Yuan shall, in accordance with law, by examination and registration determine the following qualifications:

1. For appointment as a public functionary.
2. For candidacy to public office.
3. For practice in specialized professions and as technical experts.

Article 86. The organization of the Examination Yuan shall be determined by law.

Section 6.   The Censor Yuan

Article 87. The Censor Yuan is the highest organ through which the Central Government exercises its censorial powers. It shall attend to impeachment and auditing and be responsible to the People's Congress.

Article 88. In the discharge of its censorial powers, the Censor Yuan may, in accordance with law, interrogate the various Yuan, Ministries and Commissions.

Article 89. In the Censor Yuan, there shall be a President who shall hold office for a term of three years and may be eligible for re-election.

Article 90. Members of the Censor Yuan shall be elected by the People's Congress, from candidates separately nominated by the Delegates of the various provinces, Mongolia, Tibet and Chinese citizens residing abroad. Each group of Delegates shall nominate two candidates. The candidates are not confined to Delegates to the Congress.

Article 91. Members of the Censor Yuan shall hold office for a term of four years and may be eligible for re-election.

Article 92. When the Censor Yuan finds a public functionary in the Central or local government guilty of violation of a law or neglect of his duty, an impeachment may be instituted upon the proposal of one or more Members and the indorsement, after due investigation, of five or more Members. Impeachment against the President or Vice-President, the President of the Executive Yuan, Legislative Yuan, Judicial Yuan, Examination Yuan or Censor Yuan may be instituted only upon the proposal of ten or more Members and the indorsement, after due investigation, of one-half or more of the Members of the entire Yuan.

Article 93. When an impeachment is instituted against the President or Vice-President or the President of the Executive Yuan, Legislative Yuan, Judicial Yuan, Examination Yuan or Censor Yuan in accordance with preceding Article, it shall be brought before the People's Congress. During the adjournment of the People's Congress, the Delegates shall be requested to convene in accordance with law an extraordinary session to decide whether the impeached shall be removed from office.

Article 94. Members of the Censor Yuan shall not be held responsible outside of the said Yuan for opinions they may express and votes they may cast while discharging their duties.

Article 95. Without the permission of the Censor Yuan, no Member of the Censor Yuan may be arrested or detained except when apprehended in *flagrante delicto*.

Article 96. No member of the Censor Yuan may concurrently hold any other public office or engage in any business or profession.

Article 97. The election of the Members of the Censor Yuan and the organization of the Censor Yuan shall be determined by law.

CHAPTER V.   THE LOCAL INSTITUTIONS

Section 1.   The Provinces

Article 98. In the province, there shall be a Provincial Government which shall execute the laws and orders of the Central Government and supervise local self-government.

Article 99. In the Provincial Government there shall be a Governor who shall hold office for a term of three years. He shall be appointed and removed by the Central Government.

Article 100. In the province, there shall be a Provincial Assembly which shall be composed of one member from each district or municipality to be elected by the district or municipal council. Members of the Provincial Assembly shall hold office for a term of three years and may be eligible for re-election.

Article 101. The organization of the Provincial Government and the Provincial Assembly as well as the election and recall of the Members of the Provincial Assembly shall be determined by law.

Article 102. The government of areas not yet established as provinces shall be determined by law.

Section 2.   The Districts

Article 103. The district is a unit of local self-government.

Article 104. All matters that are local in nature are within the scope of local self-government.

The scope of local self-government shall be determined by law.

Article 105. Citizens of the district shall, in accordance with law, exercise the powers of initiative and referendum in matters concerning district self-government as well as the powers of election and recall of the District Magistrate and other elective officials in the service of district self-government.

Article 106. In the district, there shall be a District Council, the members of which shall be directly elected by the citizens in the District General Meeting. Members of the District Council shall hold office for a term of three years and may be eligible for re-election.

Article 107. District ordinances and regulations which are in conflict with the laws and ordinances of the Central or Provincial Government shall be null and void.

Article 108. In the district, there shall be a District Government with a District Magistrate who shall be elected by the citizens in the District General Meeting. The Magistrate shall hold office for a term of three years and may be eligible for re-election.

Only those persons found qualified in the public examinations held by the Central Government or adjudged qualified by the Ministry of Public Service Registration may be candidates for the office of District Magistrate.

Article 109. The District Magistrate shall administer the affairs of the district in accordance with the principles of self-government and, under the direction of the Provincial Governor, execute matters assigned by the Central and Provincial Governments.

Article 110. The organization of the District Council and District Government as well as the election and recall of the District Magistrate and the Members of the District Council shall be determined by law.

Section 3. The Municipalities

Article 111. Unless otherwise provided by law, the provisions governing self-government and administration of the district shall apply *mutatis mutandis* to the municipality.

Article 112. In the municipality, there shall be a Municipal Council, the Members of which shall be directly elected by the citizens in the Municipal General Meeting. One-third of the Members shall retire and be replaced by election annually.

Article 113. In the municipality, there shall be a Municipal Government with a Mayor to be directly elected by the citizens in the Municipal General Meeting. He shall hold office for a term of three years and may be eligible for re-election.

Only those persons found qualified in the public examinations held by the Central Government or adjudged qualified by the Ministry of Public Service Registration may be a candidate for the office of Mayor.

Article 114. The Mayor shall administer the affairs of the municipality in accordance with the principles of municipal self-government and, under direction of the competent supervising authority, execute matters assigned by the Central or Provincial Government.

Article 115. The organization of the Municipal Council and Municipal Government as well as the election and recall of the Members of the Municipal Council and the Mayor shall be determined by law.

CHAPTER VI. NATIONAL ECONOMIC LIFE

Article 116. The economic system of the Republic of China shall be based upon the Min Sheng Chu I (Principle of Livelihood) and shall aim at national economic sufficiency and equality.

Article 117. The land within the territorial limits of the Republic of China belongs to the people as a whole. Any part thereof the ownership of which has been lawfully acquired by an individual or individuals shall be protected by, and subject to the restrictions of law.

The State may, in accordance with law, tax or expropriate private land on the basis of the value declared by the owner or assessed by the Government.

Every landowner is amenable to the duty of utilizing his land to the fullest extent.

Article 118. All subterranean minerals and natural forces which are economically utilizable for public benefit, belong to the State and shall not be affected by private ownership of the land.

Article 119. The unearned increment shall be taxed by means of a land-value-increment tax and devoted to public benefit.

Article 120. In readjusting the distribution of land, the State shall be guided by the principle of aiding and protecting the land-owning farmers and the land-utilizing owners.

Article 121. The State may, in accordance with law, regulate private wealth and enterprises when such wealth and enterprises are considered detrimental to the balanced development of national economic life.

Article 122. The State shall encourage, guide and protect the citizens' productive enterprises and the nation's foreign trade.

Article 123. All public utilities and enterprises of a monopolistic nature shall be operated by the State; except in case of necessity when the State may specially permit private operation.

The private enterprises mentioned in the preceding paragraph may, in case of emergency for national defense, be temporarily managed by the State. The State may also, in accordance with law, take them over for permanent operation upon payment of due compensation.

Article 124. In order to improve the workers' living conditions, increase their productive ability and relieve unemployment, the State shall enforce labor protective policies.

Women and children shall be afforded special protection in accordance with their age and physical condition.

Article 125. Labor and capital shall, in accordance with the principles of mutual help and cooperation, develop together productive enterprises.

Article 126. In order to promote agricultural development and the welfare of the farming population, the State shall improve rural economic and living conditions and increase farming efficiency by employment of scientific farming.

The State may regulate the production and distribution of agricultural products, in kind and quantity.

Article 127. The State shall accord due relief or compensation to those who suffer disability or loss of life in the performance of military or public services.

Article 128. The State shall give suitable relief to the aged, feeble, or disabled who are incapable of earning a living.

Article 129. While the following powers appertain to the Legislative Yuan in the case of the Central Government, they may be exercised by the legally designated organ if, in accordance with law, such matters may be effected independently by a province, district or municipality:

1. To impose or alter the rate of taxes and levies, fines, penalties, or other imposts of a compulsory nature.

2. To raise public loans, dispose of public property or conclude contracts which increase the burden of the public treasury.

3. To establish or cancel public enterprises, monopolies, franchises or any other profit-making enterprise.

4. To grant or cancel public enterprises, monopolies, franchises or any other special privileges.

Unless specially authorized by law, the government of a province, district or municipality shall not raise foreign loans or directly utilize foreign capital.

Article 130. Within the territorial limits of the Republic of China all goods shall be permitted to circulate freely. They shall not be seized or detained except in accordance with law.

Customs duty is a Central Government revenue. It shall be collected only once when the goods enter or leave the country.

The various grades of government shall not collect any dues on goods in transit within the country, with the exception of tolls levied for the purpose of improving the waterways and roads, on vessels and vehicles making use of them.

The right to impose taxes and levies on goods belongs to the Central Government and shall not be exercised except in accordance with law.

CHAPTER VII. EDUCATION

Article 131. The educational aim of the Republic of China shall be to develop a national spirit, to cultivate a national morality, to train the people for self-government and to increase their ability to earn a livelihood, and thereby to build up a sound and healthy body of citizens.

Article 132. Every citizen of the Republic of China shall have an equal opportunity to receive education.

Article 133. All public and private educational institutions in the country shall be subject to State supervision and amenable to the duty of carrying out the educational policies formulated by the State.

Article 134. Children between six and twelve years of age are of school age and shall receive elementary education free of tuition. Detailed provisions shall be provided by law.

Article 135. All persons over school age who have not received an elementary education shall receive supplementary education free of tuition. Detailed provisions shall be provided by law.

Article 136. In establishing universities and technical schools, the State shall give special consideration to the needs of the respective localities so as to afford the people thereof an equal opportunity to receive higher education, thereby hastening a balanced national cultural development.

Article 137. Educational appropriations shall constitute no less than fifteen per cent of the total amount of the budget of the Central Government and no less than thirty per cent of the total amount of the provincial, district and municipal budgets respectively. Educational endowment funds independently set aside in accordance with law shall be safeguarded.

Educational expenditures in needy provinces shall be subsidized by the central treasury.

Article 138. The State shall encourage and subsidize the following enterprises or citizens:

1. Private educational institutions with a high record of achievement.

2. Education for Chinese citizens residing abroad.

3. Discoverers or inventors in academic or technical fields.

4. Teachers or administrative officers of educational institutions having good records and long service.

5. Students of high records and good character who are unable to pursue further studies.

CHAPTER VIII. THE ENFORCEMENT AND AMENDMENT OF THE CONSTITUTION

Article 139. The term "law" as used in the Constitution means that which has been passed by the Legislative Yuan and promulgated by the President.

Article 140. Laws in conflict with the Constitution are null and void.

The question whether a law is in conflict with the Constitution shall be settled by the Censor Yuan submitting the point to the Judicial Yuan for interpretation within six months after its enforcement.

Article 141. Administrative orders in conflict with the Constitution or laws are null and void.

Article 142. The interpretation of the Constitution shall be done by the Judicial Yuan.

Article 143. Before half or more of the provinces and territories have completed the work of local self-government, the Members of the Legislative Yuan and of the Censor Yuan shall be elected and appointed in accordance with the following provisions:

1. The Members of the Legislative Yuan: The Delegates of the various provinces, Mongolia, Tibet, and of the citizens residing abroad, to the People's Congress shall separately hold a preliminary election to nominate half of the number of the candidates as determined in Article 67 and submit their list to the People's Congress for election. The other half shall be nominated by the President of the Legislative Yuan for appointment by the President.

2. The Members of the Censor Yuan: The Delegates of the various provinces, Mongolia, Tibet, and of the citizens residing abroad, to the People's Congress shall separately hold a preliminary election to nominate half of the number of candidates as determined in Article 90 and submit their list to the People's Congress for election. The other half shall be nominated by the President of the Censor Yuan for appointment by the President.

Article 144. The Magistrates of districts where the work of self-government is not yet completed shall be appointed and removed by the Central Government.

The preceding paragraph is applicable *mutatis mutandis* to those municipalities where the work of self-government is not yet completed.

Article 145. The methods and procedure of helping the establishment of local self-government shall be determined by law.

Article 146. No amendment to the Constitution may be made unless it shall have been proposed by over one-fourth of the delegates to the People's Congress and passed by at least two-thirds of the delegates present at a meeting having a quorum of over three-fourths of the entire Congress.

A proposed amendment to the Constitution shall be made public by the proposer or proposers one year before the assembling of the People's Congress.

Article 147. In regard to those provisions of the Constitution which require further procedure for their enforcement, such necessary procedure shall be determined by law.

NATIONAL SALVATION MANIFESTO (1936)[1]

On May 31, 1936 the following statement was adopted at the convention of the All-China Federation of National Salvation Unions. It is a statement of principles and program, expressing the desire of the patriotic movement for internal unity and resistance to Japan.

Since "September 18th" China has experienced four years and eight months of suffering. During this period Japanese imperialism has on the one hand blinded the powers of Europe and America with the smokescreen of the establishment of a military base for an attack upon the Soviet Union. On the other hand it has lured our authorities into the trap of "joint suppression of Communism," at the same time that it seizes from us a territory of 1,680,000 square kilometres, covering six provinces, enslaving sixty million of our people, and killing more than 300,000.

Since last November, Japanese imperialism has continued its march for the acquisition of the five provinces of North China. In view of the fact that North China is extremely important, because of its resources, for our national defense, and since Japanese imperialism always marches forward one foot after gaining an inch, while our authorities retreat further and further thus creating the conditions for our complete enslavement, the students of Peiping, in defiance of the bombers and guns of the enemy launched the militant demonstrations of December 9th and 16th. Since that time, the patriotic movement has spread to every section of the country, and has developed to include all strata of society. Because of the incessant struggle of the National Salvation front, there was a temporary alleviation of the situation in North China, and the activities and propaganda of the traitors were prevented from appearing in the open.

In the past five months, the National Salvation front has repeatedly pointed out: The main function of the continental policy of Japan is to attain enslavement of the whole of China and the only way for us to save our country from this enslavement and to struggle for existence, is to immediately unite the whole country, and to use all of our forces for a war of resistance against the enemy. The National Salvation front has repeatedly advocated: All military units of this country should put an end to civil war,

[1] Reproduced in *Voice of China* (Shanghai), June 15, 1936, pp. 7-8, 21-22.

which kills our own countrymen and wastes our national strength, and take prompt action to unite to fight the enemy. We have advocated that all such shameless slogans that teach the people to be pro-enemy and which destroy the national morality, such as "co-operation," "friendliness" and "peaceful relations with other states" be given up, and that freedom of speech and freedom of anti-enemy organizations be granted to the people; that correct international relations be readjusted, so as to ally ourselves with those nations who have common cause with us, and who treat us as equals.

The developments of the past five months prove that our estimation is correct and that our demands are reasonable. Now Japanese imperialism is proceeding still further with its unified aggression. It has increased its garrison force in North China, surpassing the conditions stipulated by the so-called Tangku Agreement, which is regarded by us a . . . disgrace and humiliation. . . . Its naval and military force openly protect smuggling, which is used as a bait to enlarge the camp of the traitors, thus causing bankruptcy of the law abiding merchants and the national industry.

We are broken hearted when we think of our fellow countrymen in the Northeast and in North China, who are exposed to random massacre, arrests, tortures, ravishment and insult by the enemy! We despair when we think of the various authoritative groups inside the country, who under the swords of the enemy, continue to kill each other and waste the strength of the nation! Had there not been continuous civil warfare in the past four years and eight months, we would not have to speak today of preparation! Had we been able to unite internally in the face of the intensification of external aggression, our enemy could have been made to tremble. Unfortunately the authoritative groups in the country have continued to strive for power, though they are situated on a melting mountain of ice. They are unfolding their desire for leadership in the shadow of the guillotine! They ignore the danger of the nation, the jeering of the enemy and the wrath of the people!

The facts before us are very plain! In the past four years and eight months the Western Powers under their erroneous policy of assisting Japanese imperialism to invade the Soviet Union, have been rewarded by fatal threats to their interests in the Far East; and our own pro-Japanese bureaucrats, under their false policy of permitting Japanese imperialism to build an anti-Soviet base in the Northeast, and of dreaming of the erection of an international anti-Communist league with Japan, are in danger of destroying the life of the whole nation!

The bloody teachings of the past four years and eight months, and the appeals and activity of the National Salvation front in the past five months have awakened the consciousness not only of the majority of the people, but also of the sincere elements among the various authoritative groups. Many of the comparatively advanced political leaders do realize that continuation of civil strife . . . only works to weaken the strength of the nation and helps to fan the flame of the enemy.

Unfortunately, while the majority thoroughly understand the situation, a few who have other interests still consider the Soviet Union and the Communist Party as the main enemies of the Chinese nation, and believe that the Sino-Japanese dispute may be amicably settled through diplomatic means.

While the enemy is intensifying its aggression, and internal warfare is still continued, all people are eagerly hoping for a national united front for the cause of national salvation. Driven by this demand, delegates from national salvation bodies of various circles from all parts of the country have come to Shanghai for the inauguration of the All-China National Salvation Federation, and for the formation of a united peoples' National Salvation front.

In the inauguration meeting we openly criticized the past errors of the various parties and groups, and also frankly criticized the past errors of the National Salvation Front. The aim of this criticism is to correct these errors and to prevent their recurrence, but not at all to attack or defeat any influence. We declare wholeheartedly to the nation: With the exception of traitors, we do not wish to see the slightest loss of influence of any group; we want to foster them, unite them and strengthen them, and to turn them into a mighty force to fight against Japanese imperialism.

The Conference regards the protest launched against the smuggling activities of Japanese and Korean ronins and the publication of documents concerning the increase of Japanese forces in North China, and of the full text of the Tangku Agreement, as comparatively acceptable diplomatic deeds. But when protest proves of no avail, what is then to be done?

The Conference considers: As a modern country, the Central Government should not devote itself to the unification of its power, while it neglects the duties required of a unified power—principally the task of national defense. The local governments should not enjoy the profits of the land and blood and sweat of the people during ordinary times, and neglect their obligation to protect the territory and the lives and properties of the people in time of emergency. When the enemy invades our territory, the local authorities should realize that . . . it is their inescapable duty to fight desperately against the enemy for the defense of the country. And the Central Government also must figure out a plan and mobilize the whole nation, regardless of regional differences, to fight the enemy. It should not regard the matter as one of local nature. So, we firmly demand: the authorities of North China, in the face of the most critical situation, must determine to live or die with the land and the people. On the other hand, the Central Government must also determine to start a new life with the people.

In connection with present North China situation, we, therefore, advocate: 1. To mobilize a country-wide struggle to cope with the North China situation; 2. To immediately mobilize the whole country to break off economic relations with Japan, to fundamentally suppress smuggling and to carry on a war of resistance.

The Conference agrees in principle to the theory of the Central authorities for sincere consolidation for struggle against the national crisis. But while on the one hand the slogan is put forward, on the other the ignoring of external aggression is advocated, so that internal opposing elements may be eliminated by means of civil war. This is not only a theoretical contradiction, but in practice it is impossible. The Conference considers: So long as the country is in a most critical position, prejudicial action disregarding common welfare only incurs opposition from the people.

The Conference considers: At present practically none of the various parties and groups can in a short period achieve the annihilation of other parties and groups. Immediately after the January 28th Event, the Central Government promised that it would be able to suppress the Communist Party in six months. As a matter of fact, after a period of more than four years, with hundreds of thousands of heroic fighters, who would otherwise be anti-Japanese warriors, killed in action, and unmeasured ammunition wasted, a situation of deadlock continues to exist between the two fighting bodies, and the whole nation has been made powerless to resist the enemy! No authoritative group can succeed in annihilating all other groups, without exhausting its own strength and becoming captive to Japanese imperialism.

The Conference considers that all authoritative groups committed ... errors in the past; these errors can be corrected only in the action of sincere co-operation in unanimously fighting against the enemy. The Conference thinks the political leadership will go to those who meet the demands of the people in ordinary times and who earnestly lead in the anti-Japanese war at the present moment. If our greatest enemy is condoned but force of arms is used to conquer other parties and groups, the result will be nothing but loss of the confidence of the people and self-destruction! The Conference considers that both economically and militarily, the Central Government is in the best position, and that politically it has the greatest responsibility. Therefore it is the Central Government that must receive the most severe criticism from the people and from whom the people have the most eager expectation. The Conference considers that the past error of the Central Government lies in the fact that it abandoned the task of national revolution and devoted itself to the conquest of the whole of China by means of force; that its present error lies in the fact that it has externally neglected the common enemy of the nation, and internally has made a last stand with its national defense force for the suppression of its opposing groups. For the sake of the whole nation, we do not want to see more of our force consumed in internal strife, and particularly we do not wish to see the Central Government adhere to its erroneous policy, thus wasting more of its superior force. Only if the Central Government can correct its past errors, take up the task of national revolution anew, and particularly lead a serious war of resistance against Japan, can it be free from its worry about its leading position, both militarily and politically. Only in this way can the Central Government acquire and maintain leadership.

The Conference considers: at present evidence shows the possibility of consolidating the country. General Li Tsung-jen recently showed his determination to fight against Japan at all costs; General Feng Yu-hsiang recently advocated a stop to the civil war, alliance with the Soviet Union and joint resistance against Japan; the Chinese Communist Party also revised a part of its political program so as to manifest its sincerity to fight jointly with other parties and groups against the Japanese. The Conference considers that it is the unanimous demand of all sides that China needs a national revolution to struggle for independence and liberation. The point of dispute in the past was only the method by which this national revolution can be achieved. This problem can be settled now under the demand for a war of resistance against Japan, as the first principle in common.

The Conference considers that it was only natural that in the past mutual suspicion and vigilance existed among the various parties and groups in their strife for political hegemony. For this reason, civil warfare has continued and joint action outward has been impossible. The existence of the deadlock has caused every person who has concern for the affairs of state to be sorrowful and has caused the nation to be permanently in the abyss of civil warfare. The most urgent task of the national salvation front is to break this deadlock, and the national salvation front alone has the power to break it, to promote the formation of the joint anti-enemy front by the various parties and groups, and to bring revival to the nation. The Conference, therefore, sincerely proposes to the various parties and groups:

1. That all parties and groups immediately put an end to civil war;

2. That all parties and groups immediately free the political prisoners in their custody;

3. That all parties and groups immediately send formal delegates, through the National Salvation Front of the people, to begin joint negotiations, so as to formulate the joint anti-enemy program and to build a united anti-enemy political power.

4. That the National Salvation Front of the People will guarantee with all the force at its disposal, the faithful fulfillment of the anti-enemy program by any and all parties and groups.

5. That the National Salvation Front of the People will with all the forces at its disposal, use sanctions against any party and group that violates the joint anti-enemy program, and acts to weaken the united strength against the enemy.

The Conference considers that the main task of the national salvation front, to induce the various authoritative groups to jointly fight the enemy, is of historical importance. To achieve this important task it is extremely necessary that the force of the front itself be enlarged and strengthened.

The Conference seriously and frankly announces: The Peoples' National Salvation Front has no political ambition whatsoever. It does not intend to strive for political power, but wants only to perform the natural duty of the people of the nation. We do not assist any party or group to fight for leadership or for inheritance rights. Our aim is to promote the formation of a united, anti-enemy, political power. We will strive to maintain our political independence and refrain from helping one party to attack the other. Ours is a struggle for a certain policy, but not a struggle for political power.

The Conference solemnly declares: The National Salvation Front is quite willing to make sincere negotiations with the local authorities in regard to the development of the local national salvation movement; we promise to sincerely co-operate with all those authorities, regardless of our past conflicts, who permit us to proceed with our national salvation movement within a certain proper limit. We sincerely guarantee that our masses will observe the limit agreed upon in negotiations.

Undoubtedly our proposals and the carrying out of our task will frighten our enemy. It is certain that the enemy will use all its force to break our front. The Conference, therefore, sincerely advises the various parties and groups not to listen to the rumors and slanders of the enemy and not to make free use of the charge of reaction to defame the National Salvation Front of the people. In the meantime, the Conference guarantees: Hereafter in its speeches, the National Salvation Front will never make malicious attacks against any authorities, except that it will oppose their compromise with the enemy, their suppression of the people, of freedom of speech, their erroneous theories intended to anesthetize the people, and their "turning backward of the wheel" to place obstacles in the way of progress of the nation. Rumors, slanders and demagogy are weapons needed only by the reactionary enemies in the course of their debacle.

The Conference considers that a war of resistance staged by the great Chinese nation against Japanese imperialism will encourage the whole world. The existence of Japanese imperialism is not only a great threat to the peace of mankind, but is a monster in the eyes of human morality. The peoples of the world who are struggling for peace, humanity, truth and righteousness, will understand that the anti-Japanese war of China is not only for the existence of the Chinese nation, but for the removal of the common enemy of the human race. It will be a war of international co-operation to sweep away the monster, with the Chinese nation functioning as the vanguard. The masses of the world . . . not only will extend their warm support to us, but should also take a heroic part in this international war against the common enemy. The Conference knows that in the past, many organizations in the various countries have had connections with the Chinese Peoples' National Salvation Front and have given us support. The Conference suggests to the masses of the world, including the rational people of Japan: Those who have not yet established connection with the Chinese Peoples' National Salvation Front, should immediately establish such connections with us. We ask all experts, strategists, writers, journalists who are interested in this international war, to keep in constant communication with us: We heartily welcome your participation; you can exert a mighty force in foreign lands as well as in China.

The Conference sincerely announces to the nations of the world: All countries who have the good will to support China in its struggle against Japan, will receive the warmest welcome from the Peoples' National Salvation Front, which will regard them as friendly nations. As soon as China is victorious in the anti-Japanese war, she will be a new independent state. This new state will observe the interests of all foreign countries in China with the exception of the enemy aggressor, which alone will be cancelled. The new state will need much assistance from the various countries in its reconstruction. The various nations can expect more investment and trade and more effective protection in China, when the new China will be in a position to offer a foundation of peaceful development for them. The Conference appeals to the various countries: Please do not listen to the high-sounding words of Japanese imperialism any more. You cannot expect to maintain or develop your interests in China under the protection of the international monster that disregards good-faith and truth. You have been deceived in the past.

You will incur even greater losses, should you actually gain some of the robbers booty, for that would only call forth opposition from the Chinese people.

The internal consolidation of China for a united struggle against Japan is the only condition which will bring permanent peace in the Far East; and on the foundation of permanent peace alone can you maintain and develop your reasonable interests!

The Conference believes that its fresh, impartial, frank and righteous attitude can work to turn the National Salvation Front into the greatest force of the people at the present stage, and can successfully bring into realization the historical task of accomplishing the sincere consolidation for struggle against the national crisis. The establishment of this correct attitude will not only gain the nation-wide confidence of the people but will also strengthen mutual confidence of the various groups. The Conference expects that the whole body will acquire a new encouragement spiritually and new vitality in the action of the marching forward for the accomplishment of our task of consolidation, and that it will open a new era for the National Salvation front and build a new foundation for the Chinese nation. The National Salvation Front has a pure motive. The task of National Salvation is a glorious one. The whole body with this new policy must with the utmost frankness and earnestness bring our proposals forward to all the people of the nation. Without hesitation and without fear, we must appeal straightforwardly to the masses of the people, for the final great victory.

MANIFESTO ON SEIZURE OF CHIANG KAI-SHEK (1936)[1]

This "Telegram to the Nation" was issued from Sian on December 12, 1936 by Chang Hsueh-liang, Yang Hu-cheng, Yu Hsueh-chung and other leaders of the Northwest. It is a statement of their motives and objectives in detaining Chiang Kai-shek.

Ever since the loss of the North-Eastern Provinces five years ago, our national sovereignty has been steadily weakened, and our territory has dwindled day by day. We suffered national humiliation at the time of the Shanghai Truce, and again with the Tangku Truce and the Ho-Umetsu Agreement. There is not a single citizen who does not feel sick at heart because of this.

Recently there have been startling changes in the international situation. Certain Powers are intriguing with one another, and using our nation and our people as a sacrifice. When hostilities began in East Suiyuan, popular resentment reached its height, and our soldiers everywhere were very indignant.

At this juncture, our Central Leader ought to encourage both military and civilians to organize the whole people in a united war of national defence. But while those soldiers at the front endure death and bloodshed in the defence of our national territories, the diplomatic authorities are still seeking compromises.

Ever since the unjust imprisonment of the patriotic leaders in Shanghai, the whole world has been startled; the whole of our people has been filled with anger and distress. To love one's country is an offence! This is a terrifying prospect.

Generalissimo Chiang Kai-shek, surrounded by a group of unworthy advisers, has forfeited the support of the masses of our people. He is deeply guilty for the harm his policies have done the country. We, Chang Hsueh-liang and the others undersigned, advised him with tears to take another way; but we were repeatedly rejected and rebuked.

Not long ago, the students in Sian were demonstrating in their National Salvation movement, and General Chiang set the police to killing these patriotic children. How could anyone with a human conscience bear to do this? We, his colleagues of many years' standing, could not bear to sit still and witness it.

Therefore we have tendered our last advice to Marshal Chiang, while guaranteeing his safety, in order to stimulate his awakening.

The Military and Civilians in the North-West unanimously make the following demands:

[1] James Bertram, *First Act In China* (New York, Viking, 1938), pp. 126-27.

1. Reorganize the Nanking Government, and admit all parties to share the joint responsibility of saving the nation.

2. Stop all kinds of civil wars.

3. Immediately release the patriotic leaders arrested in Shanghai.

4. Release all political prisoners throughout the country.

5. Emancipate the patriotic movement of the people.

6. Safeguard the political freedom of the people to organize and call meetings.

7. Actually carry out the Will of Dr. Sun Yat-sen.

8. Immediately call a National Salvation Conference.

The eight items above are the points of National Salvation unanimously maintained by us and by all the Military and Civilians throughout the North-West.

We, therefore, hope that you gentlemen will stoop to meet public sentiment and sincerely adopt these demands, so as to open one line of life for the future, and remedy past mistakes that have been the ruin of the country. The great cause is before us: it does not permit glancing backward. We hope to carry out the policies here maintained only for the liberation and benefit of the country. As to our merit or guilt, we leave this to the judgment of our fellow-countrymen.

In sending this telegram, we urgently await your order.

Sian, December 12, 1936.

COMMUNIST STATEMENT ON UNITY (1937)[1]

This declaration of September 22, 1937 constituted an announcement to the country that Chinese unity had been restored for the sake of resistance to Japan.

Beloved Compatriots—The Central Executive Committee of the Communist Party of China respectfully and sincerely issues the following Manifesto to all fathers, brothers and sisters throughout the country or:

At the present juncture when the country is facing extreme danger and the fate of the nation is in the balance, in order to save the country from extinction, we have, on the basis of peace and national unity and joint resistance against foreign aggression, reached an understanding with the Kuomintang of China, and are determined to participate in the concerted effort for overcoming the national emergency. This has a profound significance on the future of the great Chinese nation. For we all know that, when the national existence is endangered, only through internal unity can the aggression of imperialistic Japan be overcome. The foundation of national solidarity is now already laid, and the campaign of national emancipation launched. The Central Executive Committee of the Communist Party of China congratulates itself on the brilliant future of the nation. However, in order to transform this future into the realization of a New China, independent, free and happy, all descendants of Huangti (the first Chinese Emperor) must patiently and unceasingly participate in the concerted struggle.

The Central Executive Committee of the Communist Party of China avails itself of this opportunity to propose the following general objectives for the common struggle of the entire people or:

(1) Struggle for the independence, liberty and emancipation of the Chinese nation by promptly and swiftly preparing and launching the national revolutionary campaign of resistance with a view to recovering the lost territories and restoring the integrity of territorial sovereign rights.

(2) Enforce democracy based on the people's rights and convoke the National People's Congress in order to enact the Constitution and decide upon the plans of national salvation.

(3) Improve the well-being and enrich the livelihood of the Chinese people by relieving famines and other calamities, stabilizing the people's livelihood, consolidating national defense and

[1] Reproduced in *Finance and Commerce* (Shanghai), September 29, 1937, p. 252.

economy, removing the sufferings of the people and bettering their living conditions.

These are the urgent requirements of China, for which the struggle is aimed. We believe that they will receive the whole-hearted support of the entire people. The Communist Party of China is ready to co-operate fully with their compatriots for the attainment of these objectives.

The Communist Party of China fully realizes that this programme is likely to meet with numerous difficulties. The first obstacle will come from Japanese Imperialism. In order to deprive the enemy of all pretext for aggression and dispel doubts on the part of friends, the Central Executive Committee of the Communist Party of China solemnly declares the following in connection with national emancipation:

(1) The San Min Chu-I (Three People's Principles) enunciated by Dr. Sun Yat-sen is the paramount need of China to-day. This Party is ready to strive for its enforcement.

(2) This Party abandons its policy of overthrowing the Kuomintang of China by force and the movement of sovietization and discontinues its policy of forcible confiscation of land from landowners.

(3) This Party abolishes the present Soviet Government and will enforce democracy based on the people's rights in order to unify the national political machinery.

(4) This Party abolishes the Red Army, reorganizes it into the National Revolutionary Army, places it under the direct control of the Military Affairs Commission of the National Government, and awaits orders for mobilization to share the responsibility of resisting foreign invasion at the front.

Beloved compatriots, the sincerity, honesty and faithfulness of the attitude of this Party have already been manifested before the entire people in both words and action, and have received the approval of the people. In order to secure closer unity with the Kuomintang of China, consolidate national peace and unity, and carry out this sacred revolutionary war, we have decided immediately to translate into action those parts of our words which have not yet been enforced, such as the abolition and reorganization of the Red Army in the Soviet Area, in order to facilitate unified command for resisting the enemy.

The enemy have penetrated into our country; the moment is critical. Compatriots, let our 400 million people rise and unite. Our nation, with its long history, cannot be conquered. Rise and struggle for the consolidation of national unity and overthrow of Japanese oppression. Victory will be ours. Long live the victory for resisting Japan. Long live the independence, liberty and welfare of new China.

CHIANG KAI-SHEK ON KUOMINTANG-COMMUNIST UNITY (1937)[1]

In this statement made September 23, 1937 Chiang Kai-shek commented on the Communist statement of the previous day concerning the reestablishment of Chinese unity.

The aim of the Nationalist Revolution is to seek freedom and equality for China. Dr. Sun Yat-sen said that the *San Min Chu I* are fundamental principles of national salvation. He earnestly hoped that all our people would strive with one heart to save the state from its perils. Unfortunately, during the past ten years not all of our countrymen have had a sincere and unwavering faith in the Three Principles of the People, nor have they fully realized the magnitude of the crisis confronting our country. The course of the Revolution in its efforts at national reconstruction has been blocked by many obstacles. The result has been waste in our national resources, widespread suffering among the people, increasing humiliations from outside, and growing dangers to the state.

During the past few years the National Government has been calling ceaselessly upon the nation to achieve genuine internal solidarity, and to face unitedly the national crisis. Those who have in the past doubted the Three Principles of the People have now realized the paramount importance of our national interests, and have buried their differences for the sake of internal unity. The Chinese people today fully realize that they must survive together or perish together, and that the interests of the nation must take precedence over the interests of individuals or groups.

The Manifesto recently issued by the Chinese Communist Party is an outstanding instance of the triumph of national sentiment over every other consideration. The various decisions embodied in the Manifesto, such as the abandonment of a policy of violence, the cessation of Communist propaganda, the abolition of the Chinese Soviet Government, and the disbandment of the Red Army are all essential conditions for mobilizing our national strength in order that we may meet the menace from without and guarantee our own national existence.

These decisions agree with the spirit of the Manifesto and resolu-

[1] Reproduced in Chiang Kai-shek, *Resistance and Reconstruction* (New York, Harper, 1943), pp. 20-21. In this volume the date is erroneously given as September 24, 1937 instead of September 23. Cf. *The Chinese Year Book, 1938-39* (Shanghai, Commercial Press, 1939), p. 340.

tions adopted by the Third Plenary Session of the Kuomintang. The Communist Party's Manifesto declares that the Chinese Communists are willing to strive to carry out the Three Principles. This is ample proof that China today has only one objective in its war efforts.

In our revolution we are struggling not for personal ambitions or opinions, but for the realization of the Three Principles of the People. Especially during this period of national crisis, when the fate of China lies in the balance, we ought not to argue over the past, but should try as a nation to make a new start. We should earnestly strive to unite, so that as a united nation we may safeguard the continued existence of the Republic.

If a citizen believes in the Three Principles and works actively for the salvation of the state, the Government should not concern itself with his past, but should give him opportunity to prove his loyalty in service to the Republic. Likewise, the Government will gladly accept the services of any political organization provided it is sincerely working for the nation's salvation, and is willing under the banner of our national revolution to join with us in our struggle against aggression.

The Chinese Communist Party, by surrendering its prejudices, has clearly recognized the vital importance of our national independence and welfare. I sincerely hope that all members of the Communist Party will faithfully and unitedly put into practice the various decisions reached, and under the unified military command that is directing our resistance, will offer their services to the state, fighting shoulder to shoulder with the rest of the nation for the successful completion of the Nationalist Revolution.

In conclusion, I may say that the foundation of the Chinese state rests firmly on the Three Principles first expounded by Dr. Sun Yat-sen. This foundation is one that cannot be shaken or changed. Now that the entire nation is awakened and solidly united, it will boldly follow the unswerving policy of the Government, and will mobilize the entire resources to resist the tyrannical Japanese and save the state from its imminent peril.

Enlightened people the world over now realize that China is fighting not merely for her own survival, but also for world peace and for international faith and justice.

PROGRAM OF RESISTANCE AND RECONSTRUCTION
(1938)[1]

The Extraordinary Congress of Kuomintang Delegates met in Hankow during March 29-April 1, 1938 and adopted the following declaration concerning war policy.

A. General Principles

1. Dr. Sun Yat-sen's revolutionary principles and his other teachings are hereby declared to be the supreme authority, regulating all wartime activities and the work of national reconstruction.

2. All war-time powers and forces are hereby placed under the control of the Kuomintang and of General Chiang Kai-shek.

B. Diplomacy

3. China is prepared to ally herself with all states and nations that sympathize with her cause, and to wage a common struggle for peace and justice.

4. China is prepared to safeguard and strengthen the machinery of peace as well as all treaties and conventions that have the maintenance of peace as their ultimate object.

5. China is prepared to ally herself with all forces that are opposed to Japanese imperialism in order to check Japanese aggression and to safeguard peace in the Far East.

6. China is prepared to improve still further the existing friendly relations with other Powers in order to gain more sympathy for the cause.

7. All bogus political organizations which Japan has created in consequence of her military occupation of Chinese territory, and all their actions, are hereby repudiated and declared null and void.

C. Military Affairs

8. The army shall receive more political training, so that both officers and men may appreciate the importance of war-time national reconstruction and be ready to lay down their lives for the nation.

9. All able-bodied men shall be trained; the people shall have

[1] *The Chinese Year Book, 1938-39* (Shanghai, Commercial Press, 1939), pp. 337-38.

their military strength increased; the troops at the various fronts shall be supplied with new recruits. Overseas Chinese who have returned home to offer their services at the front shall be given a proper course of training to fit them for their work.

10. All people who have arms of their own shall receive the support and encouragement of the Government and, under the direction of local military authorities, shall cooperate with the regular army to defend the country against foreign invasion. Guerrilla warfare shall be waged in the enemy's rear with the object of smashing and dividing his military forces.

11. Both the wounded and the killed shall be pensioned; the disabled shall be cared for; and the families of soldiers fighting at the front shall be treated with the utmost consideration, so that people will rejoice to fight for their country and the work of national mobilization may proceed with the highest degree of efficiency.

D. Politics

12. A People's Political Council shall be created in order to unify the national strength, to utilize the best minds of the nation, and to facilitate the formulation and execution of national policies.

13. The district shall be taken as the fundamental unit from which the work of increasing the self-defensive power of the people shall be started. The conditions of local self-government shall be fulfilled as soon as possible, so that the political and social basis of the present war shall have been firmly established and a preparation shall have been made for the eventual promulgation of a constitution.

14. A thorough reform in the central and local governmental machinery shall be instituted with the object of simplifying and making it rational. Only thus can administrative efficiency be obtained to meet the urgent needs of war.

15. The conduct of all officials, both high and low, shall conform to rules of propriety. They shall be faithful to their work, ready to sacrifice themselves for the cause of the nation, observe discipline, and obey orders, so that they may serve as a model for the people. If they prove to be disloyal and obstruct the prosecution of the war, they shall be tried by court martial.

16. Corrupt officials shall be severely punished, and their property shall be confiscated.

E. Economics

17. Economic reconstruction shall concern itself mainly with matters of military importance, and incidentally with matters that contribute to the improvement of the livelihood of the people. With these objects in view, a planned economy shall be put into operation, investments by people both at home and abroad shall be encouraged, and large-scale wartime production shall be undertaken.

18. The greatest measure of energy shall be devoted to the development of village economy, the encouragement of cooperative enterprises, the unhampered transportation of foodstuffs, the cultivation of waste land, and the work of irrigation.

19. Mining shall be undertaken; the foundations of heavy industries shall be laid; light industries shall be encouraged; and handicraft industries in the various provinces shall be developed.

20. War-time taxes shall be levied, and thoroughgoing reforms in financial administration shall be instituted.

21. The banking business shall be strictly controlled, so that commercial and industrial activities may be properly adjusted.

22. The legal tender shall be made unassailable; foreign exchange shall be controlled; and imports and exports shall be regulated in order to secure financial stability.

23. Facilities of communication shall be improved; transportation by steamers, automobiles, and aeroplanes shall be undertaken; railroads and highways shall be built; and air lines shall be increased.

24. No profiteering or cornering shall be allowed; and a system of price-fixing shall be instituted.

F. Mass Movement

25. The people throughout the country shall be organized into occupational groups such as farmers, laborers, merchants, and students. The principle shall be: From each according to his ability. The rich shall contribute in money, and the able-bodied shall sweat. All classes of people shall be mobilized for war.

26. In the course of the war, the freedom of speech, the freedom of the press, and the freedom of assembly shall be fully guaranteed to the people, provided they do not contravene Dr. Sun Yat-sen's revolutionary principles or the provisions of the law.

27. Refugees from the war areas as well as unemployed people shall receive relief, and shall be given proper training to fit them for war-time work.

28. National consciousness shall be instilled into the people, so that they may assist the Government in detecting and eradicating treasonable acts. Traitors shall be severely punished, and their property shall be confiscated.

G. *Education*

29. The whole educational system shall be reorganized. A course of war-time education shall be instituted, and emphasis shall be placed on the cultivation of morals, scientific research, and the expansion of research facilities.

30. Various technical experts shall be trained and assigned to proper posts in order to meet the requirements of war.

31. The youths of the nation shall be properly trained, so that they may offer their services to society and contribute to the cause of the war.

A LIBERAL VIEW OF THE DRAFT CONSTITUTION (1940)[1]

This manifesto of May 28, 1940 was issued by the Kwangsi Constitutional Government Advancement Association.

The movement of the Chinese people for a democratic legislative system is already forty years old. The Father of Our Country, Sun Yat-sen, and the Kuomintang that he created passed through several decades of sacrificial struggle, beyond question wishing to make of China a modern nation in which the people have, the people rule and the people enjoy. Therefore the completion of constitutional government and the achievement of popular rule are objectives that the people of the whole country have pursued for several decades—objectives that the last testament of the Father of Our Country bequeathed to the efforts of the Kuomintang and the National Government for realization.

After the success of the Northern Expedition, the Kuomintang and the National Government spent their energy in completing internal unification and economic reconstruction. There also occurred the invasion of the Japanese, who when they got an inch took a foot. Thus over ten years were wasted. Chinese politics remained in the stage of government by men; it could not enter on the usual path of rule by law and constitutional government. After the fortunate resistance of July 7, 1937 internal unity made unprecedented progress; the Three People's Principles and the Program of Resistance and National Reconstruction became political standards believed and supported unanimously by the whole nation. Nevertheless, if we really wish to bring about unity of purpose of the whole people, the gathering of our strength, and the coordination of our endeavors for resistance and establishment of the nation, we must by means of democratic rule take another step forward.

Generalissimo Chiang said in his address opening the third session of the People's Political Council: "The most powerful and stable governments in the world are certainly those that are based on the views of the people, that regard what benefits or injures the people as beneficial or injurious, and what the people see and hear as seeing and hearing." Generalissimo Chiang also said: "If we wish to achieve victory in resistance and success in establishing the nation, we surely cannot depend on military power alone, but must

[1] Translated by Lawrence K. Rosinger, with notes in "A Chinese Manifesto on Democracy," *Amerasia* (New York), October 1940, pp. 368-75.

mobilize the strength of the people and also unite their views." This was a complete and clear statement on the necessity of realizing democratic constitutional government in the midst of resistance. Therefore, last year the fourth session of the People's Political Council passed a resolution: "We petition the Government to issue an order fixing a date for summoning a National Assembly, to establish a constitution and realize constitutional government." The Sixth Plenary Session of the Kuomintang also resolved in favor of fixing a date for summoning a National Assembly to establish a constitution. These are the greatest political achievements of our resistance. They are also developments that our government and the people of the whole nation have long fervently prayed for.

Today it is not more than five months until the convention day of the National Assembly. A constitution is a great basic law to be kept faithfully by the government and the people in cooperation. Constitutional government is government under which the people have, the people rule and the people enjoy. If we wish to perfect the contents of the constitution and press forward with constitutional government under favorable circumstances, then in the process of fashioning the constitution we must exert all our strength to have the people express their opinions and participate in the formulation of views, while ourselves giving thorough consideration to the hopes and desires of the broad masses. Then it can become a constitution zealously supported by the people of the whole country. If only we have a constitution that is zealously supported by the people of the whole country, it can show the greatest effectiveness, not become a mere piece of paper.

Moreover, before our eyes the rebel Wang Ching-wei—the notorious tool of plunderers—is swindling the people, scheming to assume the false name of constitutional government, in order to conceal the reality of selling out the country, a deed whose secret dangers and shamelessness really far surpass the bribery of Ts'ao K'un. Because of this we should have the people of the whole country join in investigating the problems of a constitution and take part positively in the movement for constitutional government. Then by means of a real constitution representing public opinion, we can destroy the false constitution of a pretended public opinion; and, through constitutional government participated in by the people themselves, smash to pieces the false constitutional government that the enemy is hatching.

Now, persons from every walk of life who share this opinion— an opinion specially based on our national duty in accordance with the directives of the central government—have established the Kwangsi Constitutional Government Advancement Association, to arouse the people, aid the government and promote the work of establishing and carrying through a constitution. The Chinese Republic is really at the decisive juncture of its preservation or destruction. Moreover, the establishment of a constitution is the great plan of the nation for the coming century. Therefore, the members of this Association unanimously propose that we regard the nation as our chief consideration and the people as the fundamental standard of this, not retaining any trace of the selfish prejudice of party groups or local areas. Now, on the day of the establishment of this Association, as a matter of principle, we offer for investigation and adoption by our government and the comrades of the entire nation our views on various problems relating to the Draft Constitution of the Chinese Republic and the establishment of a constitution by the National Assembly.

Our members feel that the strength of the letter and spirit of the constitution must first of all be based on the following three principles. First, the teachings bequeathed by Sun Yat-sen, the Father of Our Country—already the common creed of all the people—must be observed without change. Secondly, the platform of the Kuomintang, the manifestos of the numerous congresses, and the Program of Resistance and National Reconstruction are pledges of the Kuomintang and National Government to the people of the whole nation and must be carried out. Thirdly, the desires and demands of the people, as reflected in the three years of resistance, must receive increasing attention.

Because they recognize these things, our members feel that the Draft Constitution of the Chinese Republic, promulgated by the National Government on May 5, 1936, although created in accordance with the teachings of the Father of Our Country and the Three People's Principles, nevertheless is not without some omissions and defects, and it is therefore surely necessary to investigate further and make additions. Among the points that are clearly most important, the first is the question of the rights of popular freedom. The rights of popular freedom—the bone and blood of democratic government—have been the most important result of the struggle of the constitutional movement in all countries. The Father of Our Country said: "A constitution is a document protecting the rights of the people." If the people's rights are not protected, a constitution is merely empty words. It is not necessary to emphasize that for over ten years, because the rights of popular freedom were not effectively protected, public sentiment sank, society was not at peace, opinions were not united, and strength on both sides declined.

The Draft Constitution of May 5, 1936, although affording protection of various rights of popular freedom, nevertheless provides that these rights can be restricted by law. This conflicts somewhat with the statement of the Kuomintang program that "the people have the right of complete freedom of assembly, association, discussion, publication, residence and belief." Our members feel that using the laws to restrict the popular freedom protected by the constitution is the same as causing the laws to diverge from the constitution. This may easily lead to malpractices. It is better to adopt the principle of direct restriction in the constitution, so that except for amendments by the National Assembly, no laws whatsoever can become additional restrictions on the rights of popular freedom. Then the constitution will be in harmony with the teachings bequeathed by the Father of Our Country and the spirit of present-day democratic politics.

The second question is that of local administration. China is a nation of great area and population. The various sections have developed very unevenly in politics, economics and culture. If we adopt a system of centralized powers and all matters, whether great or small, must await the decision of the central government, we will have the bad government that has existed since the Manchus, and this will be enough to ruin the establishment of the constitution. The Father of Our Country spoke of this in his manifesto to the nation on assuming the office of President Extraordinary of the Republic. If we adopt the system of local division of power, we will inevitably cause the splitting of the country into feudal spheres. Therefore the Father of Our Country, basing himself on the special national characteristics of our country, developed the system of balanced powers.

The seventeenth section of the *Outline of National Reconstruction (Chien Kuo Ta Kang)* declares: "In the division of power between the central government and the provinces, all matters concerning the nation as a whole must be reserved to the central government, and those concerning local administration reserved to the localities, not leaning toward centralization of power or local division of power." The first section of the Kuomintang domestic program issued in January 1924 contained the same kind of declaration. By the system of balanced powers, under which the line between the powers of the central government and the local areas is drawn in accordance with circumstances, we can avoid local parcellation and also accommodate ourselves to local development. This is really the greatest contribution of the Father of Our Country to political science.

In connection with the system of balanced powers, the province is the local unit. The central government and the provinces, in accordance with the circumstances, determine the division of authority. Besides carrying out the laws and orders of the central government and superintending local self-government, the provinces can wield political and governmental powers in dealing with local affairs. These matters have all been stated clearly in the teachings bequeathed by the Father of Our Country and in the party program of the Kuomintang. But the constitution of May 5, 1936, although providing that the provinces execute the laws and orders of the central government and superintend local self-government, nevertheless does not recognize the provinces as units of political power that exercise local governmental powers. This does not agree absolutely with the system of balanced powers.

The idea of the constitution is perhaps to avoid the impairment of national unity by local power. Who does not know that the most important objective of the system of balanced powers of the Father of Our Country is to establish firmly our national unity, by destroying at its root the anarchy in Chinese history arising from alternate strength at the center with weakness in the localities, and strength in the localities with weakness at the center. If we neglect the needs of the localities and stress formal unity, we will on the contrary bring about local parcellation. Therefore our members propose that the local system should be based entirely on the teachings bequeathed by the Father of Our Country and the program of the Kuomintang, adopting the principle of balanced powers. Governmental and political powers concerning the whole country must be in the hands of the National Assembly and the central government; governmental and political powers concerning the provinces should be in the hands of provincial representative assemblies and the provincial governments. If we divide powers between the center and the localities in this way, we will have a rational solution, and our national unity will have lasting protection.

The third question is that of the economic system. The constitution of May 5, 1936, although basing its determination of the economic system on the principle of the people's livelihood, nevertheless does not have a concrete objective. Therefore instead of the principle of the people's livelihood being clarified, confusion might easily be produced, thus bringing about social unrest. The Father of Our Country, in the principle of the people's livelihood, raised two points: the equalization of rights to the land, and the control of capital. The objective in equalizing rights to the land is to enable the tillers to have their own fields and to bring about nationalization of the land. The objective in controlling capital is to increase the capital of the state and limit the capital of the individual, in order to seek a stable sufficiency in the people's livelihood and an improvement in the living of peasants and workers. This is the essential spirit of the principle of the people's livelihood and should be expressed clearly in the language of the constitution.

Concerning the solution of various questions about the National Assembly and the execution of constitutional government, our members feel, on the one hand, that it is certainly necessary to follow the teachings bequeathed by the Father of Our Country and the domestic program of the Kuomintang and, on the other, that it is imperative to pay attention to the special circumstances and needs present in the midst of resistance. With regard to the manner of selecting delegates to the constituent session of the National Assembly, the methods of 1936 are certainly not suited to present conditions, but to have another election would surely involve difficulties.

Our members propose as a solution that the delegates and nominees selected by the central government be thoroughly representative of every anti-Japanese party, every anti-Japanese body, and every type of organ of public opinion. Every anti-Japanese army, the national minorities, and the women should have appropriate representation. Moreover, the constituent session of the National Assembly, not resting on the terms of the constitution and born entirely of the people's choice, should accept as restrictions on its powers only the boundaries set by its task of establishing and promulgating a constitution. After the promulgation of the constitution, the constituent body should be dissolved at once and the regular National Assembly elected in accordance with the provisions of the constitution. Secondly, with regard to the period of the execution of constitutional government, the constitution should be put into operation on the very day of its promulgation. From that day "the people of the whole country will in accordance with the constitution carry through the great national elections, and the National Government will, within three months after the completion of the elections, explain the official duties and transmit the administration to the government elected by the people." This is the method laid down in the *Outline of National Reconstruction*, and we should not change it. Thirdly, with regard to the method of selecting delegates to the regular National Assembly, this session should not have both elected and appointed delegates. At election time, also, the people of the whole country and the parties should have freedom of electoral competition. Then constitutional government will enter on its accustomed path.

Finally, the members of this Association wish to tell our government and our comrades of the whole country that the decision already made by the government to convene the National Assembly and realize constitutional rule should increase the enthusiastic support of the people of the whole country. The Father of Our Country and the Kuomintang struggled for several decades to realize constitutional government. Now, in accordance with the declaration of our *Tsung-ts'ai* and under the promotion of our government, one can expect announcement of the completion of the constitution on the appointed day. With cheers and enthusiasm our comrades of the entire nation should loyally and truthfully express their views on the constitution and participate positively in the constitutional movement. Thus we will show adequate respect for the views of the *Tsung-ts'ai* and realize the intentions of the government.

Politics is fundamentally a matter of ruling the people, and constitutional government is the people's politics. Therefore, in connection with the establishment of a constitution and the realization of constitutional government, it is not only the right but the duty of the people to participate. With reference to the government, it should immediately establish political equality for the people of the whole country and see to it that the people have unrestricted freedom of assembly, association, discussion and publication, so that they may be taught the idea of change. We want the constitution to have the greatest effectiveness, not to become a piece of paper, and want to give the people full opportunity before and afterwards to participate in the movement for constitutional government. Therefore the freedom of the movement for constitutional government should certainly receive increased protection from our government. To sum up: in the advancement of democratic politics and completion of constitutional government, both our government and the nation have a task: to rise in unity and strive in cooperation. The members of this Association are deeply desirous of cooperating in the work of leadership under the guidance of the *Tsung-ts'ai* and the government, together with our comrades of the entire nation, so that China may within a very brief period change from rule by men to rule by laws. Thus, in the midst of resistance, we will be able to advance the work of reconstruction, build a new China based on the Three People's Principles and at an early date achieve success. These are the objectives for which the members of this Association ardently hope.

COMMUNIST STATEMENT ON THE NEW FOURTH ARMY
INCIDENT (1941)[1]

*The following declaration of February 26, 1941 presents the Com-
munist demands resulting from the New Fourth Army incident
(referred to here as the "outrage of southern Anhwei").*

For the past twelve months, Ho Ying-chin, Chief of Staff of the
Military Commission of Chungking and head of the pro-Japanese
clique, has actively organized intrigue to surround the high government command for capitulation and carried on a 100 per cent wrong
policy of underestimating the enemy as a lesser evil than the Communists. After the international fascist Triple Military Alliance
came into existence, Ho, aided by Pai Chung-hsi of the Kwangsi
Group, attempted to form a Chiang-Ho-Pai alliance, and to entice
the Generalissimo to recognize that China's fear is not the Japanese
but the Communists. Every means has been devised and utilized to
divert the attention of the people from the war of resistance to civil
war and to stir up the feeling of the public against the Communists,
thus to pave the way for their big scale military campaign against
the Eighth Route and the New Fourth Armies. Under such circumstances, the outrage of southern Anhwei is only a natural outcome.

The outrage of southern Anhwei in which some 6000 troops and
non-soldiers of the New Fourth Army who were on their way of
withdrawal in compliance with the government order had been
slaughtered; the absurd order issued on January 17th by the Military Commission of Chungking denouncing the New Fourth as
'rebels,' disbanding the whole army and sending Commander Yeh
Ting to be court-martialed; and the further concentration of 200,-
000 Central government troops in northern Anhwei with the aim
of annihilating the remnants of the New Fourth Army in that area
constitute the most shameless deeds ever recorded in the history of
the war of resistance. These shameful actions of the pro-Japanese
elements are nothing more than to tell the enemy as well as the
whole world that anti-Communist moves have now become the first
problem of China and to suggest to the enemy: "Why not let us
be friends and join hands to fight the Communists?"

Naturally the Japanese imperialists cannot let this advantage
pass in vain. They, seeing that their greyhound Ho Ying-Chin has

---

[1] *Chinese People's Correspondence* (Manila), February 26, 1941.

obtained supreme power in the government and has achieved great success in splitting up the united anti-Japanese front, taking this rare opportunity, mobilized seven divisions of their forces on January 18th, immediately after the issue of the order of January 17th by the Chungking Military Commission, to plan a large scale offensive in Honan Province.

The Japanese offensive in southern Honan was begun on January 26th along three lines. The first group of the Japanese force consisting of four divisions started their attack from Sinyang, pushing northward along the Peiping-Hankow Railway, and captured Piyang, Wuyang, Koshan, Siping, Shanghai and Yehhsien on January 30th; the second group with one division's force is pushing westward along the Wei River and is said to have captured Shinchiu in eastern Honan; while a third group of another division of men pushes down southward from Kaifeng toward Hsuchang.

Shocked by the swift action of the Japanese, General Li Chung-jen, Commander of the Fifth War Zone, who was at the time planning the anti-Communist campaign in Chungking, had to order the troops under the command of generals Tang En-po, Li Pien-sien, Li Sien-tsau, Ho Tsu-kuo, Sun Tung-sien and Wang Tsung-len, then surrounding the remnants of the New Fourth, to move over to Honan to check the Japanese advance. This lesson has at last awakened certain Kuomintang military officers, like Tang En-po and Ho Tsu-kuo, whose past anti-Communist actions were carried on more or less by compulsion, and they are reported to have felt a little sorry for their past foolishness and gradually realized that they have fallen victims to the trap laid down by Ho Ying-chin, who since the issue of the January 17th order had gone over to Kunming and has not yet returned to Chungking ever since. Only God knows what further traitorous intrigues he is planning over there.

The Honan offensive of the Japanese has also awakened a certain portion of the Chinese people who can see now, if they could not before, the danger of the intrigue of the pro-Japanese clique, and they begin to believe that the way to re-establish the united anti-Japanese front cannot be anything else but to re-organize the Kuomintang government, driving away Ho Ying-chin and his pro-Japanese followers.

The Chinese Communist Party for the sake of safeguarding the united front and overcoming the danger of national destruction has brought forward in a determined manner the following 12 conditions as a basis for settling disputes between the Kuomintang and the Chinese Communists:

1) Immediate cessation of any provocative steps towards anti-Communist civil war;

2) Open annulment of Government orders of January 17th (order to liquidate New Fourth and Yeh Ting to be court-martialed), open apology in the name of the Government;

3) Punishment of Ho Ying-chin, Ku Chu-tung and Shan-kwan Yun-siang;

4) Immediate restoration of Yeh Ting's freedom and Yeh Ting to be reappointed as the Commander-in-Chief of New Fourth Army;

5) Immediate return of all New Fourth ammunition seized by the Government at south Anhwei and immediate release of all New Fourth prisoners taken by the Government;

6) Compensation to all the wounded and dead of the New Fourth Army south of Anhwei;

7) Immediate steps taken to stop the anti-New Fourth operation in Central China;

8) Complete destruction of blockading system along the Border Region districts;

9) Immediate release of all political prisoners including Marshal Chang Hsueh-liang, General Yang Hu-chen, and Professor Ma Yin-chu, etc.

10) Immediate abolishment of one-party dictatorship regime and improvement of administrative structure based on democratic principles;

11) To realize Dr. Sun Yat-sen's principles and obey his last will;

12) To purge all pro-Japanese groups, arrest their leaders to be court-martialed according to National Law.

The above conditions were handed over to Mr. Chang Chung, the Kuomintang representative, to be forwarded to the Generalissimo, by Chou En-lai on January 25th, but so far no definite reply from the Kuomintang has been received.

The urgent task at present is to re-establish the united anti-Japanese front but the premises of which must be the expulsion of Ho Ying-chin and his pro-Japanese clique, the withdrawal of the absurd order of January 17th, and the abolishment of the whole anti-Communist plan by the Kuomintang.

As to the future policies of the Eighth Route and the New Fourth Armies, a spokesman of the Revolutionary Military Committee of the Chinese Communist Party has made it clear in the following statement: The policy of the Eighth Route and the New Fourth Armies, he said, is to maintain the war of resistance. In order to achieve this aim, the future operations of the Eighth Route and the New Fourth Armies will co-operate with those of other anti-Japanese armies. Despite the fact that some Kuomintang troops have been fighting against the Communists, they will be still taken as friends provided they withdraw from the anti-Communist campaign, and no revenge steps of whatever nature will be taken against them. At present, with the exception of the 138th Division under the command of Li Pien-sien still stationed in eastern Anhwei to fight against the New Fourth, most of the Central troops, like those under Tang En-po, Li Sien-tsau, Ho Tsu-kuo, Sun Tung-sien and Chan Ta-ching, have already shifted to the anti-Japanese battlefields, and therefore these troops will be treated as friends as usual. As to the 300,000 troops under General Hu Chung-nan, whose anti-Japanese feeling still runs high but who was prevented from going to the front to fight the Japanese by Ho Ying-chin, the latter ordered him to station his troops in the northwest, to build up gigantic blockade lines around the Border Region, etc. General Hu when interviewed in Sian by Nan Han-sun, a representative of General Chu Teh, last December openly expressed his unwillingness to participate in the anti-Communist campaign, but "as a general," he said, "I have to obey orders." After that interview General Hu had cancelled in January his preparations to attack the Border Region, except that the blockade lines still remain and that a certain portion of his troops still attack the Eighth Route Army in the Kwan-tsung district. Whether General Hu will remain in the rear during this critical moment of the Nation or will be ordered to the front to fight the Japanese depends on the attitude of the Chungking Government.

As regards the New Fourth Army which was disbanded by Chungking but still consists of some 90,000 people, the Revolutionary Military Committee of the Chinese Communist Party feels that it is their duty to give them protection. This was why the Committee had appointed Chen Yi and Chang Yun-yih to succeed as Commander and Deputy Commander of the army. The New Fourth is now being re-organized into six divisions together with some local guerrilla detachments. The new division commanders and political commissioners will be appointed very soon. This army is now helping to organize democratic anti-Japanese powers in all the bases under their control. Those local powers are founded on the principle that Communists can hold one-third of the government posts at most while the remaining two-thirds must be distributed among members of other parties and among all anti-Japanese classes, which of course include the Kuomintang, the national bourgeoise, the anti-Japanese gentry, etc. The practice of such system which is not a policy of agrarian revolution but a policy of united anti-Japanese front is greatly welcomed by the people while at the same time all the more hated by the Japanese and pro-Japanese elements.

CHIANG KAI-SHEK ON THE NEW FOURTH ARMY INCIDENT (1941)[1]

This speech, delivered by the Generalissimo to the People's Political Council on March 6, 1941, presents the views of the Central Government on the New Fourth Army incident and subsequent developments.

I intend, as a representative of the Government, to explain today its attitude toward the conditions laid down by the Communist members of the Council. Before I make any report I wish to state that the Government did not originally intend to declare publicly its stand on its relations with the Chinese Communist Party. Now that the latter has, however, formally telegraphed these demands to the Council, which is an organ of national opinion, it has acted in a manner quite unlike that usually characterizing its words and deeds. It is, therefore, incumbent upon the Government and the Council to make a formal declaration of their attitude in the interests of the nation, the War of Resistance and the future of national reconstruction. A nation, and more especially when it is engaged in mortal combat with an aggressor, depends for its very life upon the maintenance of discipline, order and the necessity of the Government's writ being obeyed. Given a sound framework of discipline and legality it will be able to overcome whatever perils and difficulties come in its way. If, on the other hand, its military command is not unified and its authority questioned, it will meet with defeat no matter how strong its armed forces may be. We are now pitting the whole strength of the nation against the Japanese militarists in a life-and-death struggle. The fate of our nation is hanging in the balance. It is a time when we must give the most scrupulous attention to the upholding of order and authority in the State. In all matters—whether political, social or party problems—not involving conflict with, or obstruction to national order and authority, there is room for frank and open adjustment of differences in search of rational solutions. This has always been the policy and attitude of the Government in relation to the Chinese Communist Party: the achievement of unity by means of mutual concessions in the face of external aggression and the attainment of success in resistance and reconstruction.

[1] Reproduced in Chiang Kai-shek, *Resistance and Reconstruction* (New York, Harper, 1943) pp. 235-41.

I understand that the Secretariat of the Council has received two sets of demands from the Chinese Communist Party entitled: firstly, "rehabilitation measures"; and secondly, "measures for a provisional settlement"—each set containing twelve points. I can assert that though these demands were received by members of the Council before it assembled, no government institution or individual member of the Government, nor I myself, received them. Now that we have seen them we are, first of all, astonished at the wording of the titles and next, at the formal resemblance of the contents to the demands made by the Japanese prior to the Lukouchiao Incident. One is particularly and painfully reminded of the so-called "Three Principles" announced by the Japanese at that unhappy time. The Chinese Communists are as much citizens of the Chinese Republic as we all are, and yet their presentation of such demands at such a time as this would seem clearly to indicate their intention of taking up a hostile attitude to the National Government and the People's Political Council. We think, therefore, the least said the better, and do not regard it as necessary to rebut each point in detail. It is sufficient to classify the sense of the demands into three main categories of "military," "political," and "party" affairs. The first eight points of the first set of demands regarding "rehabilitation measures" and the first, sixth, seventh, eighth, ninth and tenth points of the second set regarding "measures for a provisional settlement" belong to the category of military affairs. The ninth and twelfth points of the first set and the third, fourth and fifth points of the second set belong to the category of political affairs, while the tenth and eleventh points of the first set and the eleventh and twelfth points of the second set belong to the category of party affairs. A brief explanation of the bearing of the sense of the demands under each of these three heads upon resistance and reconstruction is indispensable.

Firstly, the demand is, in effect, that the Government should not suppress disobedient and rebellious troops, that government authorities should be punished for so doing and that the losses of the mutineers in such rebellions should be compensated.

Secondly, the implication is that the Government should establish special areas outside the sphere of its authority, recognize the existence of anomalous political organizations and restrict its power to check illegal activities on the part of organizations or individuals. Recognition of a so-called "democratic authority in the enemy's rear" is also demanded. The logical outcome of all this would be disaster—such a disaster as must invariably follow any attempt by a party to take advantage of enemy invasion in order to seize supreme power.

Thirdly, the sense of the demands is that the Communist Party should enjoy a special status and special rights and that the Government should not deal with the Communist members of the Council on the same footing as it deals with all other members belonging to other parties or to none. The Government not being ready to comply, the Communists have refused to attend the present meeting of the People's Political Council. In essence this is really what the demands amount to. I think that when the Communist Party produced them it did not perhaps realize they were of so drastic a nature. But were the Government to accept them without protest, China would scarcely be any longer worthy of being called a nation or the People's Political Council an organ of the national will.

Now I shall further expound the attitude of the Government towards these three categories of demands.

In the category of military affairs the consistent policy of the Government has been to nationalize our armies. That is, under the supreme command of the National Government there is but one system of national armies, and there can be no second system of armies under the control of individual parties or private persons. I can categorically assure the Council that the national revolutionary army is the army of the State and in no way the army of any particular party whatever. It is, therefore, absolutely out of the question to regard a section of it as belonging to the Communist Party. There can be but one source of command. Should a second presume to assert itself, it would be indistinguishable from the "military council" of Wang Ching-wei's puppet regime and accordingly detested and abjured by the whole country. It is inconceivable that the Communists, if devoted to the cause of resistance, should take up such a position.

Next, the political principle of the Government is to democratize the national political system. All citizens, individually or in organized bodies, while they conform to discipline, should shoulder their responsibilities, fulfill their duties and enjoy their rights, possess all due freedom of action, but sovereignty is indivisible. If a second source of political authority were to be allowed to exist outside the Government—such, for example, as might be called by the name of a "democratic authority behind the enemy lines," mentioned in these demands—it would not differ from the traitorous administrations in Nanking and Manchuria. Not only would the Government find it intolerable, but the whole country would see in it an irreconcilable enemy.

Although as a result of the nation's historical development there is now but one party exercising administrative power, while others of varying size and permanency are "in opposition," yet all parties exist in a spirit of equality with one another, this being nowhere more markedly visible than in this democratic institution, the

People's Political Council. Here all are equal rather as citizens than as parties. There could be no room for a special status of one party or demands for special rights, such as would vitiate the sprouting of our democratic institutions. I hope that all of you councillors will fully comprehend the nature of this considered and unvarying stand of the Government regarding its relationship with political parties.

Now I would like to elaborate somewhat upon the military aspect of the matter. From the time in 1938 when the 18th Army Corps, in defiance of the orders of the High Command, arbitrarily withdrew to the right bank of the Yellow River and forcibly carried out an illegal occupation of the Sui-Teh district, the Government has been loath to consider this move as instigated solely by the Communist Party, or to hold that party guilty of sabotaging resistance; nor did it think that any such motive was necessarily behind the 18th Army Corps' insubordination. Nevertheless, the effect extended even to the rear where it created general uneasiness on account of the potential dangers it threatened. The result was highly damaging to the whole prosecution of the war, putting a weapon into the hands of the enemy and imperilling the nation in the gravest manner. During the past two years or more the Government has been simultaneously unifying the fighting efforts of the whole army at the front and stabilizing the internal condition of the nation in the southwest and northwest of the rear. It is an exceedingly distressing fact that while all other countries in the world present a united front to external aggression, with us the Government finds added to the task of waging war on an invader that of settling internal troubles. Surely such a state of affairs is not to be paralleled in the history of any other revolutionary country. However, the precautions taken by the Government have been such as to avert any disaster either at the front or in the rear and the country may reckon this as great good fortune. Despite this danger, we find our capacity to withstand the enemy strong enough to ensure our final victory and also a sound and formidable foundation laid for stability in the rear. Had it been otherwise and had timely measures not been taken, by now the provinces of the south and northwest, if not long overrun by the enemy, would have been ruined by the escapades of rebels and anti-social elements; and the people in the rear would be living in such insecurity as those suffer in provinces behind the enemy lines, in Hopei, Chahar, Shantung and Kiangsu where the National Government and its armed forces cannot protect them from the double oppression of the Japanese and the puppets.

However, the fact remains that the forces of resistance are considerably weakened by the enforced retention in the rear of large numbers of troops who might be fighting at the front. This also imposes a grievously depressing weight upon the spirits of the whole army and people. The problem is one that is really not difficult to solve. All that is required is a complete change in the attitude and actions of the Communist Party, in no longer regarding the 18th Army Corps as its peculiar possession or as an instrument for the obstruction of other sections of the national forces to the detriment of resistance. Let the Communists carry out the declaration they themselves made in 1937 wherein they said: (1) Dr. Sun's Three Principles of the People serve the needs of present-day China and the Chinese Communist Party is prepared to strive for their complete fulfillment; (2) they would abandon all violent action and policy aimed at the overthrow of the Kuomintang, the movement for the propagation of communism in China, and the policy of violent confiscation of landowners' holdings; (3) they would abolish the then Chinese Soviet government in the Northwest and work towards a united democratic government for the whole country; (4) they would abolish the name and status of the Red Army and permit its incorporation into the national revolutionary army under the command of the National Military Council of the National Government. If they would now but faithfully carry out their original intention to comply with these conditions and move all the troops connected with their party according to the plans laid down by the National Military Council into the areas appointed for them to defend, the whole country could be united to meet the invader, there would be an end of internal obstacles and anxieties, and it would be possible to deal the exhausted enemy a tremendous blow which I am convinced would bring about within a short time a most sensational victory. At least we could restore the lines held in the autumn of 1938; of this the military authorities are in no doubt. Then lost territory would be recovered and our fellow-countrymen delivered from their sufferings. This would be an immense contribution of the 18th Army Corps to the national cause and the whole country would admire the patriotism of the Communists. Our Government has no other demand to make of the Communist Party and the troops connected with it save this one fervent wish that they will carry out the obligations into which they themselves freely entered and support the Program of Resistance and Reconstruction to which the People's Political Council gave its unanimous endorsement. It merely hopes that the Communists will cast off all party prejudice and put the interests of the nation first by obeying orders, maintaining discipline and working in harmony with all their comrades-in-arms.

There are also two other groups of these demands which have an intimate relation with military affairs: what the Communists call the "prevention of provocation," the "withdrawal of the anti-Communist forces in Central China" and the "immediate cessation of all attacks on us." These three points call for some remark. This sort of senseless, mendacious, misleading and malicious propaganda vilifies our Government and deliberately injures the sacred mission of resistance, but, more than that, it offers insult to the pure spirit of the whole country's united battle against aggression. I need scarcely assert that our Government is solely concerned with leading the nation against the Japanese invaders and extirpating the traitors, and is utterly without any notion of again taking up arms to "suppress the Communists." It desires never again to hear of that ill-omened term which now has a place only in Chinese history. Let them obey orders, give up their attacks on their comrades-in-arms and cease all their provocative acts; the Government will then treat them with all possible consideration. The Government is, moreover, desirous of showing generosity and of letting bygones be bygones. In defense of our national interest it cannot, however, fail to punish and check insubordination, for it would otherwise fail in its duty to the nation. For loyal soldiers it has such a loving solicitude that the charge of provocation and attack is absurd. I can make myself responsible for the statement in your presence that at no future time could there conceivably be another campaign for the suppression of the Communists. I hope that you will address an appeal to Mao Tse-tung, Tung Pi-wu and the other Communist members of this Council to effect a change in the attitude of their party so that we can discuss here all together the questions they have raised and arrive at some reasonable solution of them. You represent the will of the nation and your bounden duty is to strive for the success of resistance and reconstruction and national unity. If the Communist Party will only accept your advice, and say and do nothing in future contrary to the Program of Resistance and Reconstruction and their own manifesto of 1937, the Government will undoubtedly respect whatever resolutions you may adopt for the settlement of the incident and see that they are carried fully into effect without delay.

In conclusion, provided unity can be preserved and resistance carried on to the end, the Government will be ready to follow your directions in the settlement of all outstanding questions. I call upon the Communist members of the Council to realize the national danger at this time of mortal combat with the invader and, acting in the spirit of the saying "brothers quarrel at home but go out together to repel assault from without," to accept the judgment of this Council and make their contribution to national solidarity. This is the fervent prayer of the whole people, and it would moreover deal the enemy a mighty blow. Out of solicitude for the Communist Party and in the desire to see it play its full part in the history of this life-and-death struggle of our country, we beg it to continue in its mission of reconstruction and resistance against aggression.

PROGRAM OF THE FEDERATION OF CHINESE
DEMOCRATIC PARTIES (1941)[1]

On March 25, 1941 the Federation of Chinese Democratic Parties was formally established. It included the National Socialist Party (unconnected with the Nazis except in name), the Young China Party, the Third Party, the Rural Reconstructionists, and the Vocational Education Group. The objectives of this combination of minor political groups are stated in the following program which was adopted in March 1941 and publicly announced on October 10, 1941.

1. To carry out resistance to the end. To recover all lost territory and fully re-establish the integrity and sovereignty of China. To oppose all movements for compromise with the invaders.

2. To embody the democratic spirit in political institutions, putting an end to one-party control over the State. Pending the enforcement of a Constitution, to establish a body representing all parties and groups for the discussion of national affairs.

3. To strengthen internal unity. All current disagreements between parties and groups to be immediately adjusted.

4. To urge and assist the Kuomintang to carry out the Outline of National Resistance and Reconstruction, determinedly and fully.

5. To establish real unity and oppose local separatism, but at the same time to define and enforce the spheres of power of the Central and local governments.

6. To insist that the army belongs to the nation, and that military men must owe loyalty to the nation alone. To oppose all party organizations in the army, and to oppose the use of the army as a weapon in party strife.

7. To enforce government by law. To protect the lives, property, and personal liberty of citizens of China and oppose all secret arrests and penalties unsanctioned by law.

8. To protect the legitimate expression of public opinion by guaranteeing freedom of speech, publication, assembly, and association.

9. To give effect to the abolition of one-party rule mentioned in Point 2, the following reforms should be made: (a) the government's prestige and influence should not be used to promote the power of any one party in schools and cultural organizations; (b)

[1] *Amerasia* (New York), April 25, 1943, pp. 104-105.

official personnel should be selected on the basis of the "best and ablest" as advocated by Dr. Sun Yat-sen, and the use of national political power for purposes of party recruiting should be prohibited; (c) the practice of paying party expenses out of National and Local Government revenues should be abolished; and (d) the "New District System," whereby members of district advisory councils and the headmen of villages are selected by examination rather than election, should be altered.

10. With reference to the current political situation, to give attention to the following points: (a) the improvement of the food, living conditions, and pay of soldiers at the front; (b) the abolition or modification of all executive orders interfering with the expansion of production; (c) strengthening the government's supervisory organs in order to put an end to all "squeeze" and corruption in carrying out State economic measures.

CHIANG KAI-SHEK ON RELATIONS WITH THE CHINESE COMMUNISTS (1943)[1]

This statement was made by the Generalissimo on September 13, 1943 to the Fifth Central Executive Committee of the Kuomintang, then holding its Eleventh Plenary Session.

After hearing the secretariat's report on the question of the Chinese Communist Party and the views expressed by various members of the Central Executive Committee I am of the opinion that first of all we should clearly recognize that the Chinese Communist problem is a purely political problem and should be solved by political means. Such ought to be the guiding principle for the Plenary Session in its effort to settle this matter. If you share my views you should maintain the policy of leniency and forbearance which we have consistently pursued in dealing with our domestic affairs with the expectation that the Chinese Communist Party will be moved by our sincerity and magnanimity no matter in what way they may slander us nor in what manner they may try to create trouble.

In spite of provocations we should abide by the manifesto of the Tenth Plenary Session: "In the case of those who sincerely believe in the Three People's Principles, obey laws and orders, do not hinder prosecution of the war, do not attempt to upset social order and do not seize our national territory in defiance of Government decrees, the Central Government would overlook their past record either in thought or in deed and should respect their opportunities, be they individuals or political groups, to serve the country." We should, now as ever, continue to be tolerant in strict conformity with the manifesto and earnestly expect the Communist Party eventually to realize and correct their errors. We should make it clear that the Central Government does not have any particular demand to make on the Chinese Communist Party but hopes that it will abandon its policy of forcibly occupying our national territory and give up its past tactics of assaulting National Government troops in various sectors, thus obstructing the prosecution of the war.

We also hope that the Chinese Communist Party will redeem its pledge made in its declaration of 1937 and fulfill the four promises solemnly announced in that document: " (1) To struggle for the

[1] *China At War* (New York), October 1943, pp. 71-72.

realization of the Three People's Principles; (2) to abandon the policy of overthrowing the Kuomintang regime by force, give up the Communist movement and discard the policy of confiscating land by force; (3) To dissolve the present government organization and by carrying into practice the principles of democracy thus help to bring about the political unity of the whole nation; (4) To disband the Red Army by incorporating it into the National Army under the direct command of the Military Council of the National Government. The troops thus reorganized will await orders to move to the front to undertake the tasks of fighting the enemy."

If the Chinese Communist Party can prove its good faith by making good its promises the Central Government, taking note of its sincerity and loyalty in carrying on our war of resistance, will once more treat it with sympathy and consideration so that we may accomplish hand in hand the great task of resistance and reconstruction.

THE KUOMINTANG CENTRAL EXECUTIVE COMMITTEE ON RELATIONS WITH THE COMMUNISTS (1943)[1]

This resolution on Kuomintang-Communist relations was passed by the Eleventh Plenary Session of the Fifth Kuomintang Central Executive Committee on September 14, 1943.

Having heard the general report on the Chinese Communist Party's activities subversive of the state and detrimental to our war effort, we realize with deep regret that the said party instead of showing the slightest sign of being moved by the generous and tolerant attitude taken by the Tenth Plenary Session held last November has actually intensified its activities of endangering the security of the state and sabotaging our war effort.

Our holy war against aggression having passed through its most critical stage after six long years, the victory anticipated by the whole nation is already in sight. In order to ensure lasting freedom and welfare for the country and final triumph over aggression, the Government is firmly convinced that unless national unity is placed on a solid foundation it is next to impossible to carry out successfully our program of resistance and reconstruction.

Bearing in mind this guiding principle, the Government sincerely hopes that the Chinese Communist Party will refrain from committing acts undermining national unity and obstructing the prosecution of our war. It is with this purpose in view that the Government has consistently taken an attitude of forbearance towards the said party.

Animated now as ever by the same spirit, we do hereby resolve to entrust the Standing Committee with the task of settling this matter and of persuading in an appropriate manner the Chinese Communists to realize their past mistakes and honestly redeem the pledge made in their declaration of September 22, 1937, namely, "One, to struggle for the realization of the Three People's Principles; two, to abandon the policy of creating disturbance and propagating the Communist movement; three, to dissolve the present Soviet government thus helping to bring about the political unity of the whole nation; four, to disband the Red army by incorporating it in the National Army under the direct command of the Military Council of the National Government."

In this way, national interests will be safeguarded, military orders

[1] *China At War* (New York), October 1943, pp. 72-73.

and Government decrees carried out, victory in our War of Resistance and success in our reconstruction work assured, so that the fervent hope of the people may be fully realized.

As the Plenary Session has resolved to convene the National Congress within one year after the cessation of hostilities to make and promulgate a Constitution, all other problems can be discussed and solved in that Congress.

The present session of the Central Executive Committee, while resolutely striving for the consummation of its fixed policy of unifying the country and safeguarding the victory of war, hereby reiterates to the Chinese Communist Party its most earnest and sincere expectations.

INDEX

Agriculture, 4-5, 32-33, 53, 82, 102
Airlines, 102
All-China Federation of National Salvation Unions, 14
manifesto of, 86-93, 95
Amoy, 65
Anhwei, Outrage of Southern, *see* New Fourth Army
Army, 9, 12, 30, 38-39, 51, 100-101, 117-119, 125
See also Red Army
Assembly, freedom of, 14, 31, 71, 102, 107, 122
Association for the Promotion of Vocational Education, 37, 57, 122

Banking, 4, 8, 12, 20, 45, 102
"Blue Shirts," 65, 66
Burma, 53
Burma Road, 37
Business, *see* Capital

"C.C." clique, 49
Canton, 17
Capital, 8, 82-83, 108
foreign, 4, 83
Censor Yuan, 58, 73, 77, 78-79, 84-85
Censorship, 41, 51
Central China, 12, 63
Central Control Committee, 10
Central Executive Committee, 10, 47, 56, 58, 60
Central Government, *see* National Government of the Republic of China
Central Hopei, 32-33
Central Political Committee, 46-47
Central Supervisory Committee, 10
Chahar, 63, 66
Chan Ta-ching, 114
Chang Chih-chung, 41
Chang Ching-hwei, 65
Chang Chun, 54
Chang Chung, 64, 113
Chang Hsueh-liang, 9, 11, 18-22, 64, 94, 113
Chang Lan, 43
Chang Yun-yih, 114
Chao Shang-tze, 66
Chen Cheng, 61

Chen Chi-tang, 17
Chen Li-fu, 61
Chen Yi, 114
Cheng Hsiao-shu, 65
Cheng Hsueh clique, 49
Chengtu, 54
Chi Hung-chang, 66
Chiang Hsiao-hsien, 65
Chiang Kai-shek, and Communists, 27-28, 39, 64-66, 96-99, 111-121, 124-125
and Constitutional Government, 60, 104-105
Japanese policy, 11, 13, 18-20, 29-30, 33-36, 51, 64-66
power and influence, 7-10, 12, 47-49, 54, 100, 109-110
seizure of, 18-24, 94-95
See also Kuomintang and National Government of the Republic of China
Chiang Kai-shek, Mme., 45, 55
Chien Kuo Ta Kang, 107, 109
China, Republic of, finances, 102
flag, 70
territory, 70
See also National Government of the Republic of China
Chinese Communist Party, *see* Communist Party of China
Chinese Soviet Republic, *see* Communist Party of China
Chou En-lai, 19, 21, 24, 29, 44, 113
Chou Pao-chung, 66
Chu Chiu-pei, 66
Chu Teh, 11, 114
Chungking, 53, 54
Civil liberties, 13, 29, 43, 71-72, 103, 106, 122
Civil service, 10, 38, 78, 81
See also Officials
Civil war, 6, 9-12, 14, 19-21, 38-44, 61, 86-87, 111
Communications, 4, 48, 54, 102
Communist Party of China, and constitutional government, 57, 60, 113
and Kuomintang, 7-13, 15-17, 19, 23, 26, 36, 38-42, 50, 61, 89, 96-99, 111-121, 124-125

THE INSTITUTE OF PACIFIC RELATIONS

The Institute of Pacific Relations is an unofficial and non-political organization, founded in 1925 to facilitate the scientific study of the peoples of the Pacific area. It is composed of autonomous National Councils in the principal countries having important interests in the Pacific area, together with an International Secretariat. It is privately financed by contributions from National Councils, corporations and foundations. The Institute, as such, does not advocate policies or doctrines and is precluded from expressing opinions on national or international affairs. It is governed by a Pacific Council composed of members appointed by each of the National Councils.

In addition to the independent activities of its National Councils, the Institute organizes private international conferences every two or three years. Such conferences have been held at Honolulu (1925 and 1927), Kyoto (1929), Shanghai (1931), Banff, Canada (1933), Yosemite Park, California (1936), Virginia Beach, Virginia (1939), Mont Tremblant, Quebec (1942). It conducts an extensive program of research on the political, economic and social problems of the Pacific area and the Far East. It also publishes the proceedings of its conferences under the title Problems of the Pacific, *a quarterly journal* Pacific Affairs, *and a large number of scholarly books and pamphlets embodying the results of its studies.*

NATIONAL COUNCILS

Australian Institute of International Affairs
Canadian Institute of International Affairs
China Institute of Pacific Relations
Netherlands-Netherlands Indies Council, Institute of Pacific Relations
New Zealand Institute of International Affairs
Philippine Institute of International Affairs
Royal Institute of International Affairs
U.S.S.R. Council, Institute of Pacific Relations
American Council, Institute of Pacific Relations

INTERNATIONAL SECRETARIAT AND PUBLICATIONS OFFICE

1 East 54th Street, New York